CW01160907

A QUINTET BOOK

First published 2002 by Krause Publications, U.S.A.
Reissued 2004 by Antique Collectors' Club Ltd, UK

Copyright © 2002 Quintet Publishing Limited

All rights reserved. No part of this publication may be reproduced, stored in a retrieval system, or transmitted in any form or by any means, electronic, mechanical, photocopying, recording or otherwise, without the prior permission of the copyright holder.

British Library Cataloguing-in-Publication Data
A catalogue record for this book is available from the British Library

ISBN 1-85149-465-0

Reissued in England by the Antique Collectors' Club Ltd, Woodbridge, Suffolk, IP12 4SD

Conceived, designed, and produced by
Quintet Publishing Limited
6 Blundell Street
London N7 9BH

Editor: Ian Penberthy
Designer: Simon Daley
Managing Editor: Diana Steedman
Creative Director: Richard Dewing
Publisher: Oliver Salzmann

Manufactured in Singapore by Universal Graphics Pte Ltd
Printed in China

NOTE: Price values are US dollars

CONTENTS

Introduction 4

1 Cars and Motorbikes 6

2 Boats 100

3 Airplanes 110

4 Other Toys 120

Further reading and Acknowledgments 127

Index 128

CARS AND MOTORCYCLES

○ ○ ○

Although in the early years Schuco was known mainly for its clockwork figures and animals, the company will be remembered best for the vast range of tinplate and diecast cars produced from the 1930s through to the 1970s, and again during the revival at the turn of the 20th century.

From the very first, relatively simple "turn-back" car of the 1930s to the huge and complicated 1950s Packard Synchromatic with automatic transmission, it was the sheer technological ingenuity that made Schuco cars so instantly recognizable. Often copied, but never equaled, Schuco's mechanical masterpieces occupy a unique position in the history of the toy car. Setting aside the limited range of modern replicas, it is unlikely that present-day or future toy cars will come close to the standards of quality, realism, play value, and durability set by Schuco. It is unusual to find even a battered 60-year-old Schuco car that refuses to run.

In the space available I have included small-scale table-top tinplate cars, Varianto track models, large-scale Mercedes and Alfa Romeo exotic sports cars, Formula One racers, and Micro-Racers (the fastest clockwork toy cars in the world), and the miniature Piccolos. That's not to ignore two wheels—Schuco produced some very fine lithographed motorcycles between the 1930s and early 1960s. Most notable was the incredible Curvo. Any one of seven different "circuits" could be "dialed" into the bike.

Today, Schuco keeps the famous name and interest alive with the regular introduction of new color schemes, reproductions of previous models, and entirely new types. Many Schuco cars have now enjoyed absolutely incredible production runs. Take the Studio Mercedes for example—first made in 1936 and to be found in the 2002 Schuco catalog, albeit with the occasional short break in production between the old Schuco, Gama and the new Schuco company. The models illustrated on the following pages are a mix of the old and the new.

COMMAND CAR

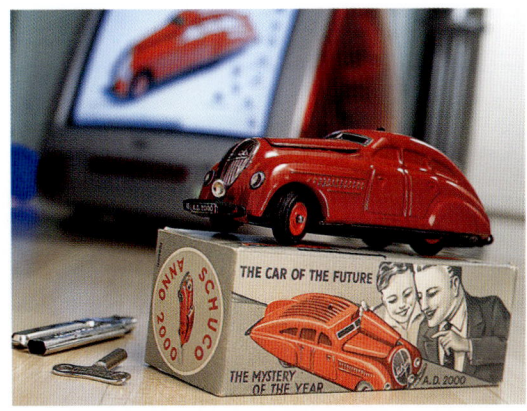

Size Length: 5.6in (142mm) Width: 1.9in (48mm)
Height: 2.4in (61mm)—hood open

Colors Mid-blue, dark blue, light green, mid-green, dark green, red, cream, maroon, turquoise

Price Mint boxed, $350

Rarity Medium ★☆

Schuco introduced this car in 1937 and called it the Car of the Future, emphasizing the point by applying "A.D.2000" to the front license plate. The box proclaimed it to be "The mystery of the year" and that "Even experts are surprised when the Schuco Command Car stops or starts on command without being touched."

The Command Car was based loosely on a 1930s Maybach. The long hood is hinged in the middle and opens to reveal a beautifully detailed, lithographed, tinplate six-cylinder engine. Schuco crammed this little car full of clever technological features. The exceptionally long-running clockwork motor, about 25 turns, enables the car to be stopped and started—using the roof lever, voice commands or the Schuco whistle—several times before rewinding is required. Beneath the roof grille is a very sensitive diaphragm that acts as a stop/start switch. Hence a blast from the Schuco whistle will cause the car to either start or stop. Voice commands work in the same way, simply relying on the speaker exhaling at the same time. Reverse gear is selected by pulling out the rear bumper. If the car reverses into a stationary object, the bumper is pushed in and the car moves forward again. This feature was designed to be used with the Schuco Command Garage (opposite). After reversing into the garage, the car mysteriously drives out again. The centrally mounted headlight can be moved to the left or right to adjust the steering of the car.

After World War II, Schuco continued to produce the Command Car until 1951. These Schucos are not too difficult to find in average condition; finding a clean working example is a little harder. The motors become sluggish with time, reverse gears slip, roof grilles are often bent, and the plating on the grille and lights is prone to corrosion. In the late 1990s, Schuco began remanufacturing the Command Car, and although not the same as owning an original, it will provide you with a very good replica.

TECHNICAL FEATURES *Very-long-running clockwork motor; reverse gear operated by pulling out the rear bumper; stop/start operated by a blast of air on the roof grille or by the roof lever; opening hood; adjustable steering by means of the central headlight.*

COMMAND CAR GARAGE

○○○

Introduced by Schuco in 1950 to accompany the Command Car, the garage is constructed from lithographed tinplate complete with corrugated roof. A slightly out-of-scale telephone is fixed to the garage wall.

The Command Car is wound up, placed in the garage, and the twin doors are shut with the door latch in place. You pick up the telephone and ask for your car to be brought out. A gentle tug on the phone cord, and the garage doors open and your car drives out, just as requested!

The Schuco Garage is fairly easy to find in good condition, although the telephone often goes missing. Schuco is remanufacturing the garage, and two different versions are available.

CARS AND MOTORCYCLES

MAGICO 2008

Although not introduced by Schuco until 1951, the Magico is very much the same as the 1937 Command Car (page 8), but a little more basic. There is no opening hood and no reverse gear. However, the stop/start diaphragm under the roof grille is straight from the latter. In place of the small roof lever, however, is a rubber antenna, which, when touched with the magic wand, either stops or starts the car. Hence the magic, as the instructions tell you, "The Mystery Car obeys GO and STOP Abracadabra commands of the young Magician, using either the magic wand or whistle. The audience will be mystified and astonished by the range of tricks the young Magician can perform. Now, just once the Schuco magician will let you apprentices in on the secrets."

The Magico has a central headlight, which, as on the Command Car, can be moved left or right to set the steering. The tinplate body is in the same 1930s style, but is unique to the Magico. Production of the original model ended in 1965, but Schuco has recently started to manufacture an excellent replica. The original Magico, having had a relatively short production run in Schuco terms, is harder to find in good condition than the Command Car, and not often found at toy sales. However, examples do surface quite often on Internet auction sites. Look out for missing rubber antennas; if the antenna is present, it is nearly always bent from the car having been kept carefully in its box.

TECHNICAL FEATURES *Usual sturdy clockwork motor; stop/start operated by a blast of air on the roof grille or a light touch of the roof antenna; adjustable steering by means of the central headlight.*

Size Length: 5.6in (142mm) Width: 1.8in (46mm)
Height: 2in (52mm)

Colors Red, gray, cream, dark green, light blue

Price Good to mint, $250–350

Rarity Quite rare ★★☆

CARS AND MOTORCYCLES

RADIO 5000

Size Length: 5.6in (143mm)
Width: 1.9in (48mm) Height: 2.2in (57mm)

Colors Red and cream, maroon and cream, dark blue and orange, dark blue and light blue (original and reissue), dark green and light green (reissue), red and maroon (reissue)

Price Mint boxed, $850–1,000 Reissue, $140

Rarity Very rare ★☆☆☆☆

This is one of the rarest and most desirable of early Schuco tinplate cars. It was introduced in 1938 and had a short production run that ended in 1943. Elegant and streamlined, its familiar art-deco styling is further enhanced by a two-tone paint job. A "technological masterpiece," as it was called at the time, it has several unusual features. It measures only 5.6 inches (143 millimeters) in length and is fitted with not one, but two clockwork motors—one to propel it, and the other to operate the musical movement, or "radio." The roof antenna also doubles as an on/off switch for the music. Pulling the antenna out starts the music; pushing it back, stops the tune.

The drive is controlled by a lever in the front window. This lever has two positions: one provides continuous drive, while the other, when used in conjunction with the radio, puts the car into a random motion. For example, with the car having been set to drive in a circle, it will make a couple of circuits, skid to a stop, with the music still playing, wait a few seconds, then start off again.

The Radio 5000 is rare and tends to be expensive when found. It is not unusual for boxed examples to fetch around $1,000 on Internet auction sites. The most likely flaw will be a bent or stretched antenna, but this is not surprising, given that it is a 60-year-old piece of fine coiled wire. Schuco did fit different music boxes to the Radio 5000, although it must be said that the tunes are not instantly recognizable. The music drum can lose teeth, making the tune even more obscure.

Schuco has recently reintroduced this model, and while the detailing on the body pressing may not be so fine, the overall appearance and paint finish is excellent. It works in exactly the same way as the original, and makes a good alternative until an original example can be found or the expense justified.

TECHNICAL FEATURES Long-running clockwork motor; clockwork musical "radio" operated by the roof antenna; stop/go mystery action; adjustable steering by means of the central headlight.

CARS AND MOTORCYCLES

13 CARS AND MOTORCYCLES

LIMOUSINE 1010

Size Length: 5.7in (146mm)
Width: 1.8in (46mm) Height: 1.9in (48mm)

Colors Red and cream, red and gray, red and maroon, light and dark blue, red, green, cream, gray

Price Original mint boxed, $350 New replica, $65

Rarity Medium ★★

Introduced in 1939, the Limousine is basically a larger version of the Patent Auto (see page 18). It has the same popular Schuco "turn back" feature. The Limousine, like the Radio 5000 (page 12), was modeled on the streamlined 1930s Maybach sedan and also was available with attractive two-tone paintwork.

Technically, the Limousine works in exactly the same way as the smaller Patent Auto, having a central driven wheel at a right-angle to the rear wheels and a weighted bulge at the front of the chassis.

In common with many Schuco cars, the Limousine had an incredibly long production run, manufacture of the original ceasing in 1965. Therefore, many have survived intact, the two-tone versions being the most sought-after. A replica from Gama appeared in 1992, and Schuco continues to produce the model today, regularly introducing new color variations.

TECHNICAL FEATURES *Robust clockwork motor; third driven wheel mounted centrally at a right-angle on the chassis, which operates the "turn back" feature.*

CARS AND MOTORCYCLES

PATENT 1250

Introduced in 1938, the Patent 1250 remained in production until 1952. In Schuco terms, it is a very basic toy car—hold the wheels, wind it up and let it go. However, it does have adjustable steering operated by a lever on the front bumper. The streamlined bodyshell, with its incredibly long hood, is shared with the much more sophisticated Fex 1111 (page 17), although with less detailing and chrome trim.

   The Patent 1250 is not too hard to find due to its long production run. The most frequent problem concerns metal fatigue of the rather delicate, diecast front bumper, and quite often the thin center section of the bumper will be missing. Clockwork motors have the usual Schuco sturdiness. At present, this model is not being remanufactured by Schuco.

TECHNICAL FEATURES
Fast and long-running clockwork motor; adjustable steering.

○ ○ ○

Size Length: 5.6in (142mm)
Width: 1.9in (48mm) Height: 1.8in (45mm)

Colors Red, maroon, gray, light green, dark green, cream, blue, turquoise

Price Mint boxed, $220

Rarity Medium ☆☆

CARS AND MOTORCYCLES

FEX 1111

The Schuco Fex dates back to 1951 and is also known as the "Höllenraser," or "Helldriver" in English. It is styled in the classic Schuco streamlined fashion and shares its bodyshell with the Schuco Patent 1250 (page 15). This car has a very special feature—the SOS button. When wound and set to run in a circle, the car behaves normally; however, pull out the SOS button at the rear, and it becomes the "Helldriver." It travels at twice the speed, rolls over, rights itself, and carries on. There are small rubber inserts in the door handles and a roof mounted "Schuco Fex" nameplate to protect the car when it rolls.

During its maneuvers, the car can take a bit of a bashing, and the paintwork does tend to suffer. The front grille and bumper, as on the Patent 1250, are rather delicate and prone to metal fatigue; often they are missing or damaged. As on most toy cars, the rubber tires can dry out with age, become hard, and lose their grip. The result is that rather than rolling over, the car will just wheelspin around in circles. Motors usually last well.

The Schuco Fex is not that difficult to find, good examples regularly cropping up in Internet auctions. Production of the original ended in 1965, but Schuco is reproducing the Fex and, again, the quality is excellent.

TECHNICAL FEATURES *Strong, long-running clockwork motor; two forward speeds—the fast speed is selected by pulling out the SOS button; adjustable steering by means of a bumper lever; an automatic brake that stops the wheels from turning before the car is placed on the floor.*

Size Length 6.0in (152mm) Width 1.9in (48mm) Height 1.8in (46mm)

Colors Red, maroon, mid-green, dark green, mid-blue, gray, cream, turquoise

Price Mint boxed, $400–500

Rarity Medium ✩✩

CARS AND MOTORCYCLES

PATENT AUTO 1001

Size Length: 4.5in (114mm)
Width: 1.5in (37mm) Height: 1.4in (35mm)

Colors Red, mid-green, dark green, gray, cream, beige, light blue, mid-blue, dark blue, turquoise

Price Mint, $120

Rarity Not rare ☆

This is a beautifully shaped, very streamlined little car, with a steeply raked front grille that gives the impression of speed even when the car is standing still. It was the first of a whole range of Schuco cars with the patented "turn back" feature. The car was designed to be used on a table-top or similar surface. Upon reaching the edge of the table, the car almost drives right over it, but at the last moment, it turns to the right and heads off toward the next edge. The car has a centrally mounted driven wheel, which runs at a right-angle to the driven rear wheels, but does not make contact with the table until the car reaches the edge. A weighted bulge in the chassis, below the front bumper, actually prevents the front wheels from touching the surface. When the car reaches the edge, the bulge drops over it, bringing the central wheel into contact with the top and causing the car to turn away. A word of warning, though; the system is not completely fail-safe and does not cope too well with round tables.

The instructions include several suggestions for using the car, including watching it go around and around on a cigarette pack! It can "also be used as a Parlor game—several cars of different colors, each player has his own color, are all wound up and all placed at the same time on a flat or round board. Any car pushed off is a loser and out of the game. The car remaining longest on the board is the winner."

These were very popular little Schucos and were sold in huge numbers between 1936 and 1952; as a result, they are not that rare. They are tough and survive well, despite the likelihood that they will have fallen off numerous tables. The rubber on the driven wheels does harden with age and flat spots occur from prolonged storage. Boxes are rare.

TECHNICAL FEATURES *Robust clockwork motor; third driven wheel mounted centrally at a right-angle on the chassis to operate the "turn back" feature.*

MIRAKO CAR 1001

Introduced in 1951, the Mirako Car is technically identical to the earlier Schuco Patent 1001, having the same "turn back" feature. The styling is very 1950s American, and the car actually resembles the popular chopped-roof "lead sled" custom cars, with its narrow windows and raked door pillars.

The Mirako Car was produced as a standard sedan or as a fire chief's car, Also available were the Mirako Bus 1004 and the Mirako Sani 1003 (ambulance), which made use of the bus and ambulance bodies from the Schuco Varianto range (pages 62 to 78). Additionally, the Mirako Car was sold with an automatic drive-thru express service station.

Boxed examples are reasonably easy to find and, again, the Internet is the best source. The fire chief's version tends to be more highly priced. There is little to go wrong on this model, corrosion of the plated parts being the only likely problem.

TECHNICAL FEATURES *Robust clockwork motor; third driven wheel mounted centrally at a right-angle on chassis to operate the "turn back" feature.*

Size Length: 4.5in (115mm)
Width: 1.5in (38mm) Height: 1.4in (36mm)

Colors Red, blue, green, cream, gray, turquoise

Price Mint boxed, $150

Rarity Medium ✩✩

CARS AND MOTORCYCLES

TELESTEERING 3000

Introduced in 1938 and continued in production with little change right through to 1960, the Telesteering car was one of the smallest and least expensive tinplate clockwork cars in the range. It was sold in such vast numbers so that it is relatively easy to find today. The Telesteering car came complete with 12 wooden posts, a wooden ball, two flags, and a steering wheel and connecting wire. The motor has four different speed settings operated by a small lever at the base of the windshield.

The instruction sheet, which states, "No more sliding about on one's knees when playing with this car," optimistically suggests several different games for the car, such as tenpins, an obstacle race, and a game where, instead of avoiding the posts, you knock them down! A form of soccer is also described: "The player who with only one winding up of the clockwork, succeeds in scoring the most goals is the winner." Not easy!

These are hard wearing Schucos with little to go wrong. The motors are strong and last well. As with any tinplate toy, corrosion is always possible, but a good complete set is not difficult to find, especially in red.

TECHNICAL FEATURES Long-running clockwork motor with four speed settings; fifth wheel mounted centrally to the front of the chassis to which the telesteering wire attaches through an opening in the hood. Early versions have "0," "I," "II," "III," and "IIII" speed markings painted on the body; later US-Zone models have these markings stamped into the body from the underside.

Size Length: 4.2in (106mm)
Width: 1.5in (38mm) Height: 1.6in (40mm)

Colors Red, maroon, mid-blue, dark blue, mid-green, dark green, turquoise, cream

Price Mint boxed, $200–250

Rarity Not rare ☆

CARS AND MOTORCYCLES

EXAMICO 4001

Size Length: 5.6in (142mm)
Width: 2.3in (58mm) Height: 2.0 in (52mm)

Colors Red, maroon, light blue, mid-blue, dark blue, mid-green, dark green, cream, gray, silver, brown, turquoise, two-tone gray and black, green and black

Price Mint boxed original, $500

Rarity Not rare ☆

The Examico dates back to 1936, the shape resembling a rather stunted BMW 328. Measuring only 5.6 inches (142 millimeters) long, it really is a masterpiece. It is powered by the usual robust clockwork motor and is equipped with a fully working four-speed transmission, complete with neutral and reverse. The gears are shifted by a dashboard mounted lever, using the same pattern as found on a real car. It even has a working clutch pedal, albeit on the outside of the car. Rack-and-pinion steering is controlled from the steering wheel, and the car also has a working hand brake. This must have been a really fascinating toy for a child during the 1930s.

Many full-size cars of the period would have had only three-speed transmissions. What would be the equivalent feature in a toy car today, satellite navigation perhaps?

This was a very successful and popular toy for Schuco, and the original production run continued without change until 1959. Many survive today, and good examples are not hard to find. The clockwork motor, as always, seldom gives up. Transmissions can become a little sticky, but a couple of drops of oil usually solve the problem. The original windshield will almost certainly have gone missing, but this is very easy to replace, merely being a flat piece of plastic that slots into the windshield posts.

The Examico was reintroduced in 1989 by Gama. Today, it is still a favorite, and Schuco regularly offers the car in new color schemes.

TECHNICAL FEATURES *Pressed-tin open-top body; long-running clockwork motor; four forward speeds, neutral and reverse; clutch for disengaging drive; rack-and-pinion steering; working floor mounted hand brake; lithographed tin dashboard with gear positions.*

23 CARS AND MOTORCYCLES

AKUSTICO 2002

Size Length: 5.6in (142mm) Width: 2.3in (58mm) Height: 2.0in (52mm)

Colors Red, maroon, light blue, mid-blue, dark blue, mid-green, dark green, cream, turquoise, two-tone dark red and black. Radio Akustico: two-tone red and black

Price Mint boxed original, $450

Rarity Not rare ☆

Introduced at the same time as the Examico (page 22), the Akustico shares the same BMW 328 bodyshell, the only difference being the absence of the clutch pedal. The Akustico actually has two clockwork motors, one for the drive, and the other for the acoustic mechanism, which is the car horn. The sound of the horn, operated by a button on the steering wheel, is made by a small hammer vibrating against a metal drum under the hood. The steering wheel also turns the front wheels by means of a rack-and-pinion system. As with the Examico, the Akustico has a working hand brake.

The Examico and Akustico are really a pair. If you have one, you should have the other. Original production ended, like that of the Examico, in 1959, but resumed with the Gama-made replica in 1989. Schuco continues to develop the model, and a version with an opening hood is now available, inspired by a prototype that Schuco produced in the 1930s. Alongside this is the Radio Akustico, which has a music box in place of the horn.

Good examples of the Akustico should not prove too difficult to find. The front grille can take a bashing, but minor dents up front on this particular model seem to give it more character.

TECHNICAL FEATURES *Clockwork driving motor; horn operated by a second clockwork motor, with winding aperture in the base of the car and giving 300 soundings of the horn from one winding; rack-and-pinion steering operated by the steering wheel; working hand brake.*

SONNY PETER 2006

Clearly, Schuco was not lacking a sense of humor when it came up with this model. Once again, the car is based on the BMW 328 and uses the Akustico 2002 bodyshell (page 24). In the driving seat is a completely mad figure, Peter, with the first ever punk hairstyle, and skinny arms with huge hands waving a balloon in the air. When wound up and on the move, Peter waves both arms up and down. The car has adjustable steering, although not linked to the steering wheel, and an automatic brake, which stops the wheels from turning until the car is put down.

The Sonny Peter was introduced in 1956 and remained in production until 1960, a very short run by Schuco standards. Consequently, this is a difficult one to find in good condition. There is another version known as the Sonny Mouse 2005, which is identical in every respect apart from the driver, which is a large mouse. Production of the Sonny Mouse began in 1952 and stopped in 1965, making it a little more common than the Sonny Peter. Both models often lose hands and balloons, while the Mouse can lose its felt ears.

TECHNICAL FEATURES *The usual robust clockwork motor, linked to the driven wheels and the driver's arms; automatic brake; adjustable steering.*

○ ○ ○

Size Length: 5.6in (142mm) Width: 3.5in (90mm)—including arms Height: 3.5in (90mm)—including hair

Colors Red, blue, mid-green, cream

Price Mint boxed, $550

Rarity Medium ★★

CARS AND MOTORCYCLES

SPORT EXAMICO AND EXAMICO SPYDER

Both of these models are new additions to the Schuco range, and not replicas based on previous Schucos, although the mechanism, dashboard and seat pressings are from the Examico 4001 (page 22). The features are identical to those of the Examico 4001, with four forward speeds, reverse and neutral, working steering and a hand brake; the absence of the clutch is the only difference. The Sport is based loosely on the Porsche 356, and the Spyder on the Porsche 550 Spyder, as made famous by James Dean. A limited-edition Police version of the Sport is also available.

TECHNICAL FEATURES
Clockwork motor with four-speed transmission; working rack-and-pinion steering operated by the steering wheel, working hand brake.

○ ○ ○

Size Length: 5.9in (150mm) Width: 2.4in (62mm) Height: 2.4in (60mm)

Colors Sport: Red, cream, white (police version) Spyder: Silver

Price About $60

RADIO AUTO 4012

Size Length: 6.1in (155mm) Width: 2.5in (63mm) Height: 2.6in (65mm)—antenna extended

Colors Blue, maroon, cream, gray, green, turquoise—all with red seats; red with green seat

Price Mint boxed, $550

Rarity Medium ★★☆

Following on from the prewar Radio 5000 (page 12), Schuco continued its fascination with car radios, obviously a great luxury at the time, and introduced the open-top Radio Auto 4012 in 1952. This is an all-time Schuco classic, and good examples will always command high prices.

Designed to resemble an early 1950s convertible, the Radio Auto, in common with other Schuco "radio" cars, has two clockwork motors—one to drive the car, and the other to power the "radio." The radio and gauges are beautifully printed on the dashboard, and within the radio is an on/off switch for the music. The sounds for the radio are provided by a Swiss musical movement. A plastic antenna on the left front fender can be raised and lowered for added realism.

Production ran for 12 years, and many have survived. Windshields and steering wheels are often cracked or missing, but replacements can be obtained from specialists. Antennas and hand brake levers often go astray. The basic functions, as always, stand up well. Mint boxed examples regularly appear on Internet auction sites. No replica of the Radio Auto is currently being produced.

TECHNICAL FEATURES
Two clockwork motors, one for the drive and the other for the musical movement; working rack-and-pinion steering operated by the steering wheel; hand brake; pressed tin body and dashboard; plastic steering wheel and seat.

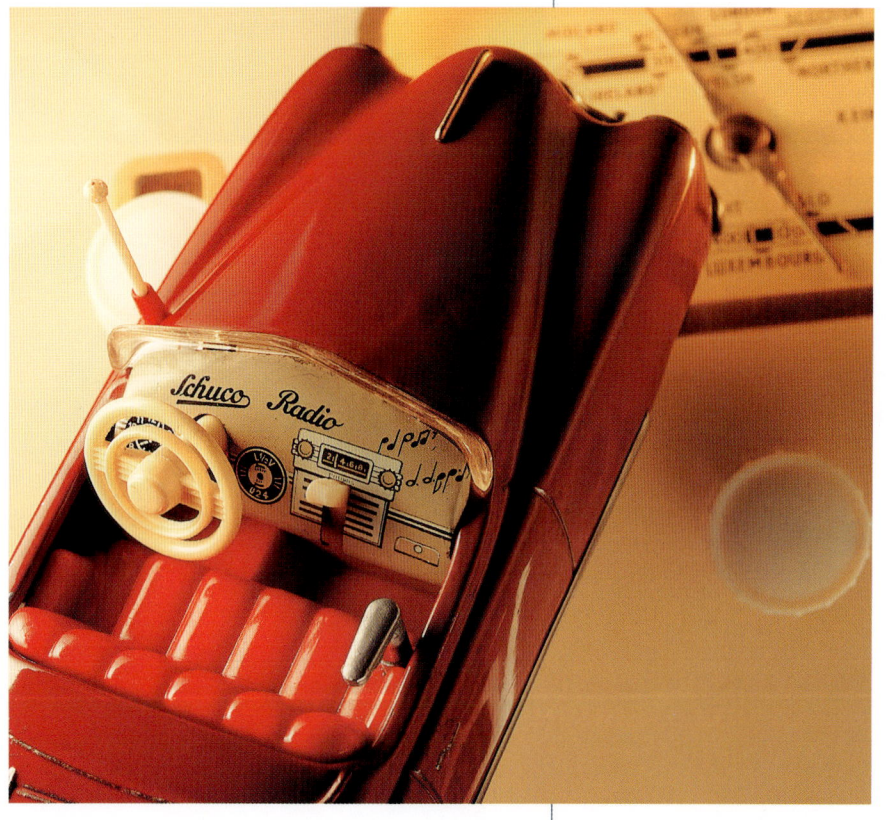

TACHO-EXAMICO 4002

The Tacho Examico was introduced in 1951 and has the same body, grille, and bumpers as the Radio Auto 4012 (page 28). The Tacho is another fine example of Schuco's wonderful obsession with realism. This little car is equipped with a column gearshift, working steering, a hand brake and a speedometer. The Tacho has three forward speeds plus reverse and neutral. The gearshift has to be pushed, pulled and moved up and down to engage the gears, just like the real thing. With neutral engaged, the car will idle realistically. The gearshift mechanism is attached behind the dashboard to the speedometer, and the needle will move relative to the gear selected.

Only produced between 1951 and 1956, the Tacho is now quite a rare find. Broken windshields and steering wheels are common, but, as with the Radio auto, replacements are available. The speedometer needle is often missing on poorer examples. Mint Tachos do crop up on the Internet, but they are sought after, which is reflected in high prices.

Size Length: 6.1in (155mm) Width: 2.5in (63mm) Height: 2.4in (61mm)

Colors Red, mid-green, mid-blue, maroon, cream, gray, turquoise

Price Mint boxed, $600

Rarity Rare ★☆☆☆

TECHNICAL FEATURES
Clockwork motor with three forward speeds, reverse and neutral; column gearshift linked to speedometer; rack-and-pinion steering operated by the steering wheel; hand brake; pressed tinplate body and seat; lithographed dashboard.

GAMA·SCHUCO 100

Although not actually made by Schuco, the 100 was an important collaboration between two of Germany's most respected toy makers, Gama and Schuco. Inspired by a late 1940s Buick, the car features the Schuco patented "turn back" feature and a "bump and go" action, which makes it turn away from any solid obstacle it bumps into.

Manufactured in fairly large numbers between 1950 and 1956, the Gama-Schuco 100 is relatively easy to find in good condition. Both company logos are lithographed on the base. As with all tinplate toys, corrosion of the plated parts is quite common. The rubber on the right-angled driven wheel hardens with age and loses grip. Best check that it doesn't fall off the edge of the table before you show it to your friends.

TECHNICAL FEATURES *Clockwork motor; on/off switch on left side of hood; Schuco patented "turn back" feature; Gama "bump and go" action.*

Size Length: 6.2in (158mm) Width: 2.8in (70mm) Height: 2.3in (58mm)

Colors Red, black, pale green, dark blue, metallic blue, cream

Price Mint boxed, $280

Rarity Not rare ☆

CARS AND MOTORCYCLES

INGENICO

Size Length: 8.7in (220mm)
Width: 3.5in (90mm) Height: 3.0in (75mm)

Colors Red, maroon, light blue, mid-blue, dark blue, turquoise, green, cream, two-tone orange and cream, two-tone light blue and cream. Also, a chrome plated version was offered

Price Mint boxed, standard single model, $550
Mint boxed, De Luxe two-car kit, $1,200

Rarity Not rare ☆

The Ingenico, introduced in 1952, was inspired by a 1951 Buick V8. This is a nicely detailed model, complete with rear fender trim, hood ornament and the familiar Buick trademark "portholes" on the front fenders. It could be purchased as a clockwork model (the 5300) or battery powered (the Elektro-Ingenico 5311). A Cabrio version of each model was also available. The Elektro-Ingenico has a separate container for the batteries, designed to be carried in the driver's pocket. This is connected to a remote steering device, which also houses the controls for forward, stop, and reverse. The hood ornament is attached to the steering mechanism and turns in the same direction as the front wheels.

Over the years, Schuco introduced various accessories for the Ingenico, notably the Carreto 5330 trailer and a lighting kit. The rear bumper on all Ingenicos is fitted with a towing hook, and the Carreto can either be used to

CARS AND MOTORCYCLES

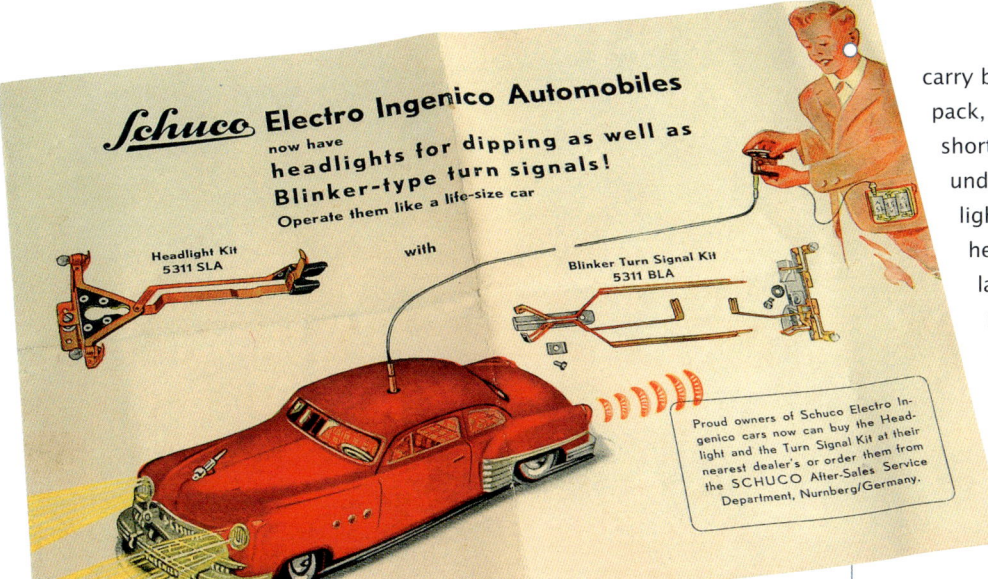

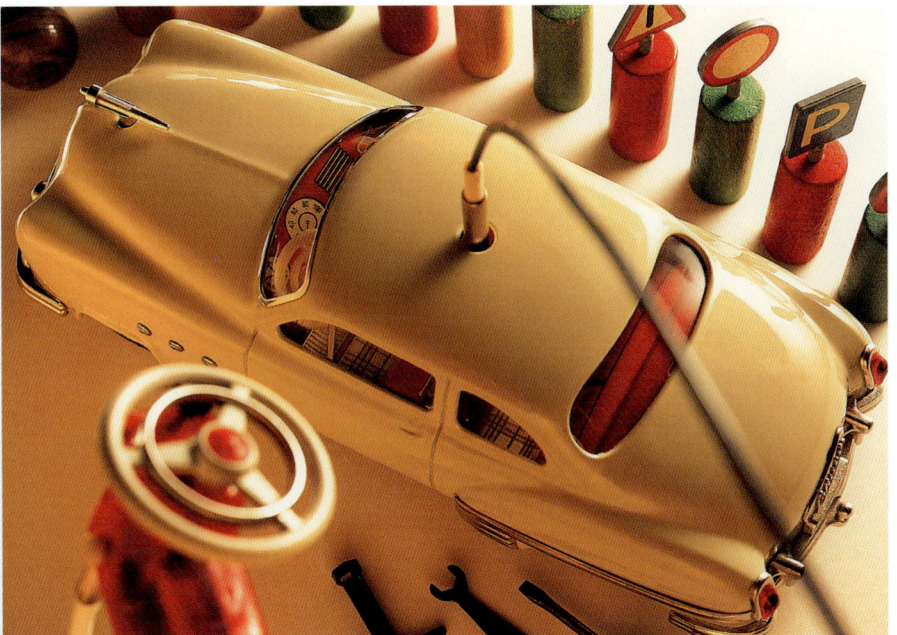

carry bits and pieces, or to hold the battery pack, which then can be connected by a short wire to an outlet on the trunk lid, underneath the sliding Schuco logo. The lighting kit gives the car working headlights and rear turn signals, the latter flashing appropriately as it steers. Both the clockwork and electric motors were available as separate items.

Ingenicos are plentiful, and a good example should not be that difficult to source. The hood ornament, being a small and removable item, often will be missing. Check the motor housing of the electric version. This is a clear plastic molding and, with age, it suffers a lot of stress cracking and eventually will fail. The correct batteries are now very difficult, if not impossible, to find. A De Luxe kit was available, which contained both the sedan and Cabrio bodies, often in very attractive two-tone paintwork. The Ingenico was facelifted in 1961 and given a new front grille, side chrome trim, and new rear license plate surround.

TECHNICAL FEATURES *Pressed painted tinplate body; diecast front and rear bumpers; lithographed tinplate interior; clockwork or battery powered motor; remote battery pack and steering wheel.*

COMBINATO 4003

Size Length: 7.6in (194mm)
Width: 3.1in (80mm) Height: 2.8in (70mm)

Colors Red, maroon, cream, mid-blue, mid-green

Price Mint boxed, $500

Rarity Medium ★★☆

The Combinato from 1953 is very much a larger version of the earlier Tacho Examico (page 30). As the name suggests, it has a combination of favorite Schuco features. It is equipped, as Schuco put it, with an "In-line gearshifting lever at the steering wheel for 3 forward and 1 reverse speeds, plus neutral, just as with a modern life-size model. With speedometer, the indicator of which shows the speed that is in mesh as well as the peak speed attainable, similar to a real car. With horn button for actuation of a special built-in, clearly audible signal device for 400 horn signals each when wound once." The horn mechanism works in the same way as that of the popular Akustico 2002 (page 24) and is operated by a second clockwork motor.

The Combinato is a perfect example of Schuco quality and obsession with realism. This would have been a very special toy when new and very likely quite expensive, which would explain why excellent boxed examples can still be found. The first item to suffer any damage is usually the windshield, but as with the Radio and Tacho cars, replacements can be obtained from specialist restorers.

TECHNICAL FEATURES *Pressed and painted tinplate body; diecast front and rear bumpers; lithographed tinplate dashboard; tinplate seat; two clockwork motors; 3 forward speeds, reverse and neutral; working horn; working rack-and-pinion steering; working hand brake.*

CARS AND MOTORCYCLES 34

EXAMICO 11

The Examico 11 is an updated version of the familiar Examico 4001 (page 22) and has the same bodyshell as the Combinato. However, it does have a different front grille and bumper, and a very attractive badge on the hood with the Schuco name and a miniature Ingenico car. Technically, the Examico 11 is identical to the Examico 4001, having a clockwork motor and four-speed transmission with a dashboard mounted shifter. The lithographed dashboard has some very fine, early 1950s styling details.

The Examico 11 was manufactured between 1957 and 1968, and toward the end of that period, tin toys had lost much of their popularity. As a result, this model is more difficult to find than the Combinato for example, which makes it a very collectable Schuco.

TECHNICAL FEATURES *Pressed and painted tinplate body; tinplate grille and bumpers; lithographed dashboard; clockwork motor; four forward speeds, neutral and reverse; rack-and-pinion steering; working hand brake.*

Size Length: 7.6in (194mm) Width: 3.1in (80mm) Height: 2.8in (70mm)

Colors Red, mid-blue, mid-green, beige

Price Mint boxed, $550

Rarity Rare ★☆☆☆

CARS AND MOTORCYCLES

MERCEDES ELEKTRO PHÄNOMENAL 5503

Size Length: 8.7in (220mm)
Width: 3.6in (92mm) Height: 2.8in (70mm)

Colors Red, mid-green, cream

Price Mint boxed, $450

Rarity Medium ✰✰

The Elektro Phänomenal, introduced in 1955, was the first of many Schuco large-scale models of the attractive Mercedes 190 SL. As the name implies, Schuco clearly thought that this was something very special – indeed it is.

Battery powered, the Phänomenal could be "gassed up" using the Schuco Gasoline Pump 5506 (available in either Shell or Aral colors). The instructions state that you should "Start filling her up only after baby cell shows signs of weakening. The car should be gassed up for approx. 5 minutes at a time (Never longer!). This will make the car run for another 30 minutes. During charging the hood with the battery inside should be kept closed. Only after approx. 100 running hours a new baby cell will become necessary. This means that 1 service hour will cost less than a fraction of a cent!" The pump locates into the right-hand rear fender.

The single battery is located under the hood, which even has its own release button on the dashboard. The electric motor is mounted at the rear of the chassis, and the trunk lid opens so that you can see what's going on. The pressing and fit of the lid is superb. A column gearshift allows forward, neutral and reverse to be selected. The car is equipped with rack-and-pinion steering, which can either be controlled from the steering wheel inside the car or remotely with a separate wire and steering wheel. Included with the car were some colored wooden poles, and the instructions suggested different ways of using these, such as "Running the Gauntlet—drive through a narrow lane with five poles on each side being placed one and a half car lengths apart. Each pole left standing is good for one point."

The Phänomenal is Schuco at its very best, and a popular model with collectors. Expect to pay a high price for a mint boxed example. Green and cream cars will usually cost more than the common red versions. Windshields have a strange habit of bending in the middle after time. However, they can be straightened with gentle and careful use of a hair dryer.

TECHNICAL FEATURES *Pressed and painted tinplate body with opening hood and trunk; lithographed tinplate dashboard; plastic seats; battery powered motor; column gearshift; rack-and-pinion steering with remote option.*

CARS AND MOTORCYCLES   38

MERCEDES CONTROL CAR 2095

The Mercedes 2095 was the second Schuco car to be based on the 190 SL cabriolet body. Much more basic than the Phänomenal (page 36), the 2095 is a simple clockwork car with remote rack-and-pinion steering. Although neither the hood nor trunk opens, the bodyshell pressing and proportions are truly excellent. An automatic brake prevents the rear wheels from turning until the car has been set down.

Since the Mercedes 2095 was made in great numbers between 1956 and 1969, finding a good one should not be too difficult. A kit version, the Montage Mercedes 2097, is much rarer, but if you find one, your dilemma will be whether or not to assemble it. Schuco reintroduced the Mercedes 2095 in 2001, and 2002 was due to see the return of the Montage Mercedes kit. Where possible, the new models have made use of the original tooling.

TECHNICAL FEATURES *Pressed and painted tinplate body; lithographed tinplate dashboard; plastic seats in red, beige, or green depending on car color; clockwork motor; automatic rear brake; remote-control steering.*

Size Length: 8.7in (220mm)
Width: 3.6in (92mm) Height: 2.8in (70mm)

Colors Red, mid-green, cream, silver (replica)

Price Mint boxed, $300

Rarity Not rare ☆

CARS AND MOTORCYCLES

ELEKTRO RAZZIA 5509

Introduced in 1958, the Razzia is one of many Schuco tinplate Mercedes 190 SL models. This hardtop version was available as a police patrol car and as a fire chief's car, and is unusual in that it is both battery and clockwork powered. The car contains two diecast figures, the driver and his partner, who holds a radio mike in his right hand. When the clockwork motor is wound, the officer raises and lowers the mike as though talking on the radio. At the same time, the roof light illuminates, and the bulb and holder actually rotate. Two 1.5 volt batteries, housed under the hood, power the car's driving motor. The hood is opened by turning the spotlight. The steering can be adjusted with the lever on the front bumper.

The Razzia is one of the rarer versions of the Schuco Mercedes 190, so good examples can be quite expensive. The red fire chief's car is the more unusual of the two. Look out for missing roof light covers. The small bulb is still obtainable, but since the whole assembly rotates, the electrical contacts often need cleaning.

Size Length: 8.7in (220mm) Width: 3.6in (92mm) Height: 3.6in (92mm)

Colors Green and white, white, red and white, red

Price Mint boxed, $600

Rarity Quite rare ☆☆☆

TECHNICAL FEATURES *Pressed and painted tinplate body; lithographed tinplate interior; diecast driver and partner; opening hood; battery powered driving motor; roof light; clockwork motor to operate the rotating roof light and move the officer's arm; adjustable steering.*

CARS AND MOTORCYCLES

ROLLYVOX 1080

Introduced in 1957, the strangely named Rollyvox uses the Mercedes 190 SL body, but with some subtle changes designed to make it look less like a Mercedes and perhaps a little more American. These changes are mainly to the hood, which no longer has the opening lines and to the front grille. The hood also has a very large, rocket-shaped ornament. The dashboard, however, is exactly the same as the Mercedes 2095 (page 39). Unusually, the Rollyvox has friction powered flywheel drive, although a clockwork motor is also provided to power the Akustico-type horn on the steering wheel.

Although production ran until 1969, today the Rollyvox is actually quite rare and therefore sought after. In common with any of the Schuco Mercedes 190 SL models, the windshield is often bowed. Currently, the model is not being remanufactured by Schuco.

TECHNICAL FEATURES *Pressed and painted tinplate body; lithographed tinplate dashboard; plastic seats; flywheel drive; clockwork powered horn; rack-and-pinion steering operated by the steering wheel.*

Size Length: 8.7in (220mm)
Width: 3.6in (92mm) Height: 2.8in (70mm)

Colors Red, cream, mid-green, mid-blue, turquoise

Price Mint boxed, $425

Rarity Rare ★☆☆☆

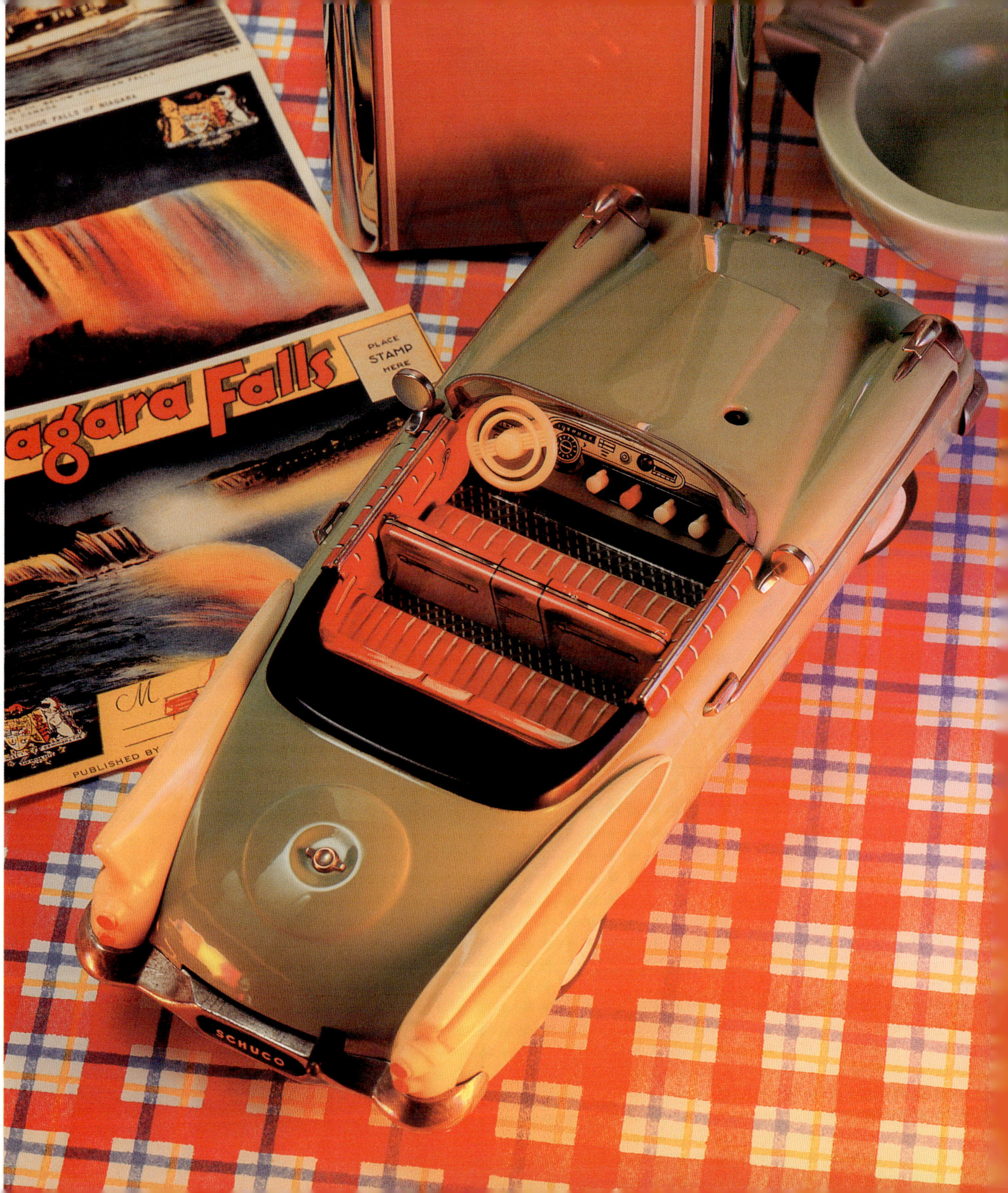
agara Falls
PLACE
STAMP
HERE
PUBLISHED BY
SCHUCO

PACKARD ELEKTRO-SYNCHROMATIC 5700

The Packard Synchromatic is arguably the finest of all the large-scale Schuco tinplate cars. Modeled on the 1957 Packard Hawk, actually not a particularly popular car, which was dropped in 1958 along with the Packard name, this huge model—10.6 inches (270 millimeters) long—is beautifully detailed. Schuco called it "The car for the up-to-date young motorist!" and fitted it with the "latest push-button gearshift." Gears can be selected manually, using the buttons on the dash, or the car can be put into fully automatic mode, using the lever at the base of the trunk lid. In automatic mode, the Packard will start by idling, then first gear is selected, followed by overdrive, stop and reverse. After this, the cycle is repeated. With each change of gear, a small red light illuminates on the instrument panel.

As the name suggests, the car is battery operated, employing rechargeable batteries that are charged with the Schuco Gasoline Pump 5506, which hooks into the car's fuel filler for a realistic effect. There are some wonderful details on the Packard, particularly the front headlight assemblies and door mirrors. The gold Packard lettering on the hood is actually mounted through very neat little cutouts in the metal.

In terms of Schuco collecting, this is the expensive end, and good Packards do not come cheaply. However, they tend to be looked after well, and generally the only potential problems are perhaps slight tarnishing of the plated parts and missing gold paint on the plastic rear fender fins. The Packard Synchromatic was made from 1958 to 1969. A rarer Elektro-Radio car was produced between 1959 and 1963, utilizing the same bodyshell with minor changes to the hood and grille. It is highly unlikely that the Packard will ever be reproduced due to the complexity of the model and the higher production costs of the much shorter runs of replicas.

TECHNICAL FEATURES *Pressed, painted tinplate body; lithographed tinplate interior and dash; plastic fins; battery powered electric motor; push-button transmission; automatic drive action accomplished by camshaft and gears; instrument-panel light; steering operated from steering wheel or by remote steering wheel and wire.*

Size Length: 10.6in (270mm) Width: 4.4in (112mm) Height: 3.4in (86mm)

Colors Red, cream, light green—all with white and gold fins

Price Mint boxed, $850

Rarity Quite rare ☆☆☆

CARS AND MOTORCYCLES

DALLI 101

The Dalli is ultimate in the long line of Schuco "turn back" cars. This one, like the Sonny Peter (page 26) is also totally mad. The car was inspired by the boat-tail version of the 1960s Alfa Romeo Spider. The oversized driver (Dalli?), a 1960s student type with turtleneck sweater, baseball cap, and glasses, occupies both front seats.

On reaching the edge of a table or flat surface, he raises his hands and turns his head, as if to say, "Look, no hands!" Then the car turns away from the edge and drives off with the driver once again holding on to the steering wheel. The box illustrations depict the young driver showing off to his friends.

Complete Dallis, in good condition, are quite rare. The first item to become damaged is always the baseball cap, the bill of which will often be missing or have been glued back in place, due of course to Dalli falling off the table and landing on his head. Entire bodies can easily become detached. However, good preserved examples can be found, and they really are quite unique, if a little eccentric.

TECHNICAL FEATURES *Clockwork motor incorporating the familiar Schuco "turn back" mechanism with right-angled driven wheel—when weight is transferred to this wheel, the driver's body is connected to the motor by a series of gears, causing him to perform his arm and head movements; pressed tinplate bodyshell, lithographed interior; plastic-bodied figure.*

Size Length: 6.5in (165mm) Width: 2.9in (73mm) Height: 3.1in (80mm)—to baseball cap

Colors Red or cream car, yellow or green sweater, yellow or green baseball cap

Price Mint boxed, $490

Rarity Rare ★☆☆☆

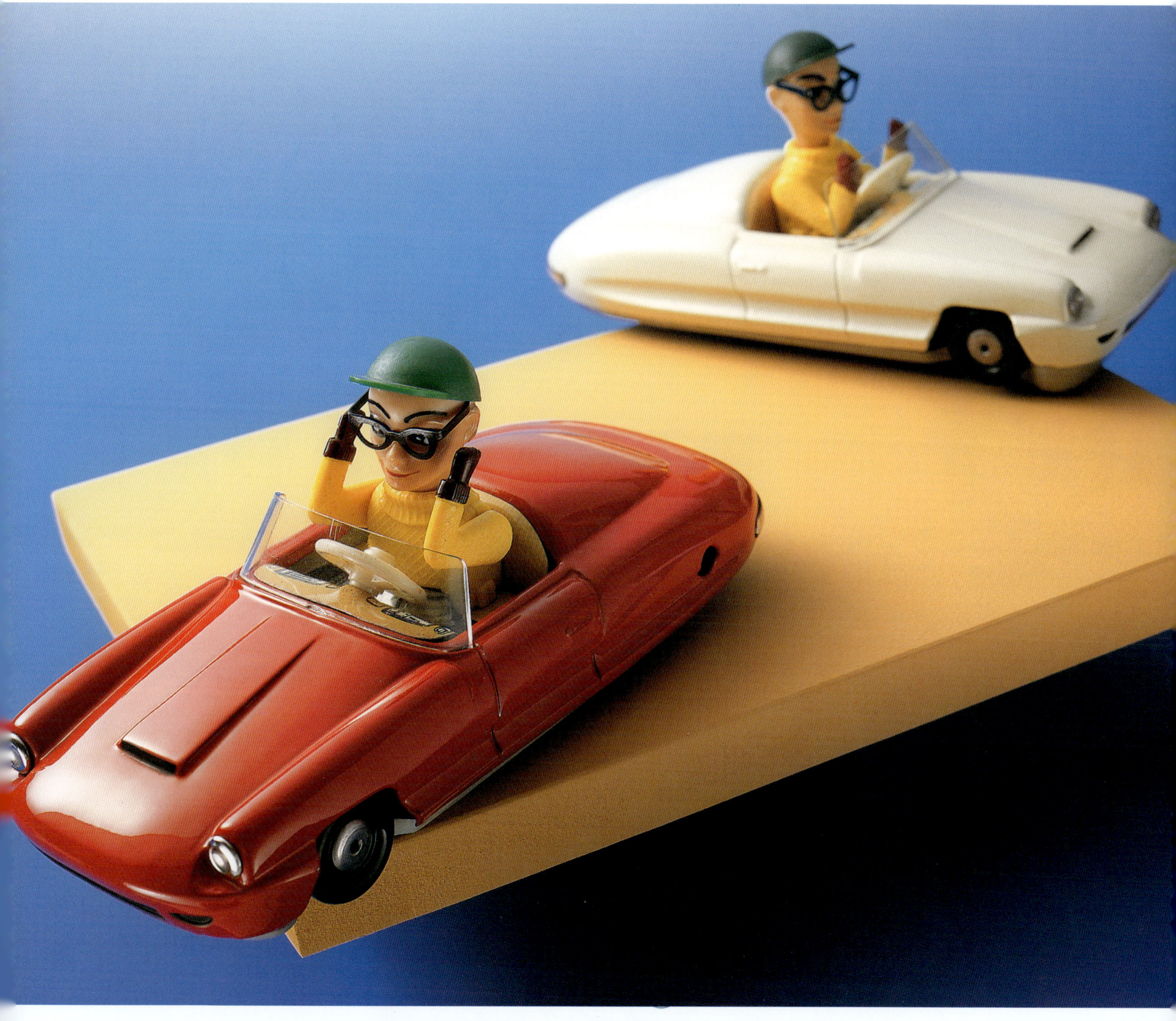

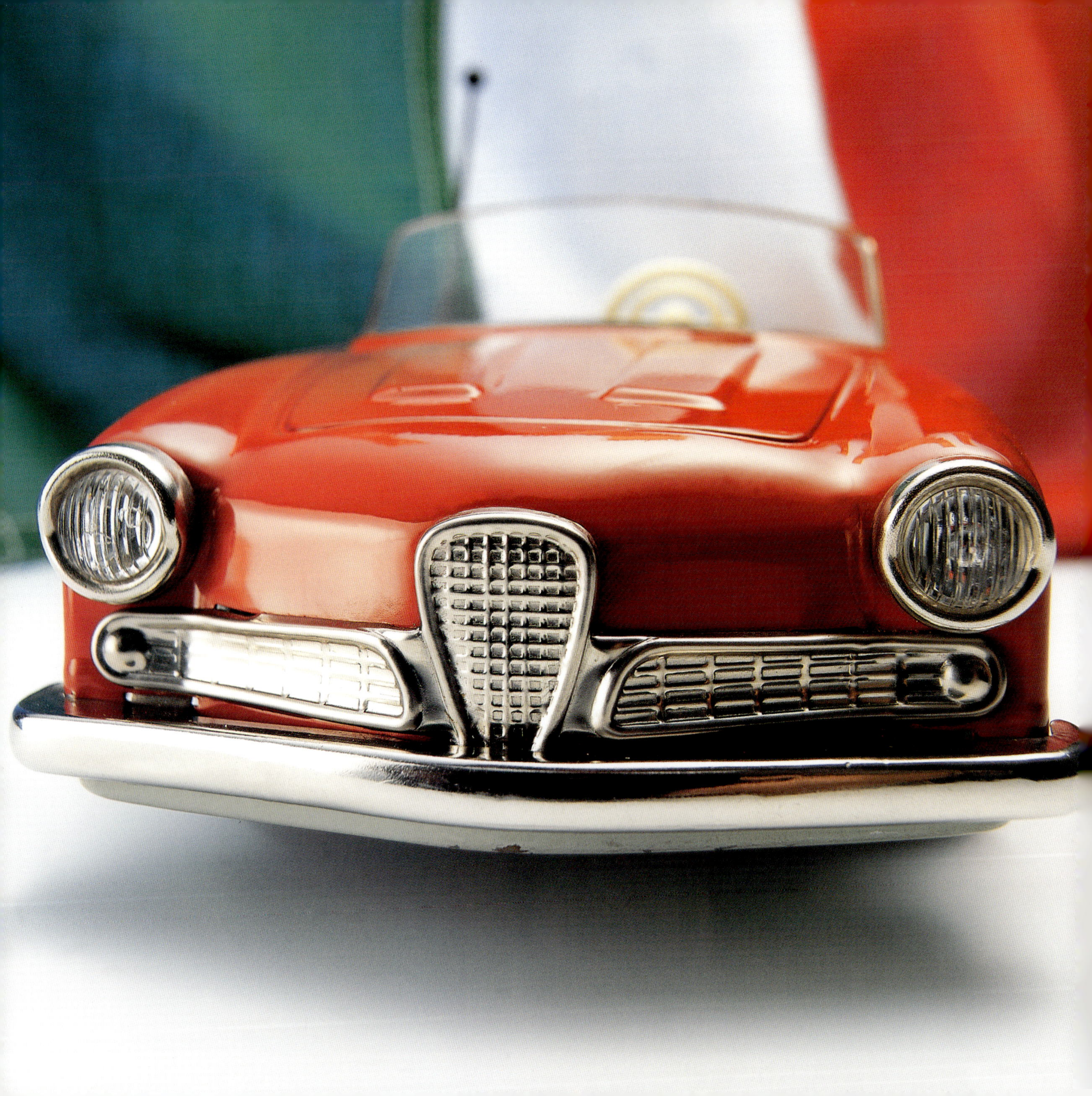

MAGICO ALFA ROMEO 2010 AND TEXI 5735

These beautiful, large-scale tinplate Schucos are based on the gorgeous Italian Alfa Romeo Giulietta. Introduced in 1964, the Magico Alfa Romeo continued and concluded Schuco's fascination with magic and mystery, following the theme of the 1950s Magico 2008 streamlined sedan. Clockwork powered, it can be started and stopped by touching the antenna, or with the magic wand provided, or by touching or blowing on the lightly weighted rear shelf. The Alfa may also be steered remotely or by using the car's steering wheel.

Employing the same body as the Magico Alfa Romeo, the Texi 5735, from 1960, is an absolutely fabulous toy even by Schuco standards. It is a clockwork powered car complete with a young blond female driver or, more rarely, the driver of the Dalli (page 44). The driver's left arm holds the steering wheel, while the right holds the column gearshift. When set on automatic, Texi will perform a figure-eight, stopping at the intersection point and going into reverse. During these maneuvers, the driver will turn to look in the direction in which the car is traveling. For example, when backing up, the driver will appear to select reverse, then actually turn around and look to the rear! The box graphics show the Alfa and young blond driver surrounded by admiring onlookers.

Both versions of this Alfa are quite scarce in comparison to, say, the Phänomenal (page 36) and accordingly are sought after by collectors. It is rare for unloved Texis to crop up in Internet auctions. In common with many of the large Schuco vehicles, they tended to be cared for and loved by their original owners. Like many of us, the blond's hair can become a little thin and frizzy with age!

TECHNICAL FEATURES *Magico: pressed and painted tinplate body; lithographed dashboard and interior; clockwork motor; stop/start by using the antenna or applying light pressure to the rear shelf; rack-and-pinion steering with remote facility.*

Texi: clockwork motor; automatic figure-eight drive pattern; driver's arms and head move in tandem with the car.

Above Texi downshifts to take a tight bend.

Left Alfa Romeo Magico

Size Length: 9.6in (245mm) Width: 3.7in (95mm) Height: 3.0in (75mm)—excluding driver/antenna

Colors Magico: red, cream, mid-blue
Texi: red, cream

Price Magico: Mint boxed, $650 ,
Texi: Mint boxed $850

Rarity Magico: rare ★★★☆
Texi: rare ★★★☆

CARS AND MOTORCYCLES

OPEL ADMIRAL ELEKTRO ALARM CAR 5340/1

AND OPEL ADMIRAL CONTROL CAR 5309

The Opel Admiral, introduced in 1967, was certainly one of the very last Schuco cars to be constructed from tinplate in an age when plastic had taken over in toy production. The Opel Alarm car is very similar to the earlier Ingenico-bodied Alarm Car, and is complete with flashing roof light, an audible alarm and a battery powered motor. One switch controls the drive, light, and alarm. This offers the options of drive alone, drive with light, or drive with light and alarm. The car also has the well-tried Schuco remote steering.

The Opel Admiral Control Car is basically a civilian version of the Alarm Car. It differs in that it has reverse gear, takes a smaller size of battery, and has no alarm or flashing light.

The fact that both models were only produced between 1967 and 1969 does make them quite scarce. However, for some reason, they are not particularly popular with Schuco collectors, which helps to keep prices at a reasonable level. Nonetheless, they are well made, save for the chrome plating, which is very thin and tarnishes easily.

TECHNICAL FEATURES *Pressed and painted tinplate body with diecast door handles; lithographed tinplate interior; battery powered motor; remote steering facility located on the hood.*

Size Length: 8.7in (220mm) Width: 3.5in (88mm) Height: Control Car, 2.8in (70mm); Alarm Car, 3.5in (90mm)

Colors Alarm Car: green with white roof, white Control Car: white, red

Price Mint boxed, $280

Rarity Alarm Car: medium ✫✫
Control Car: rare ✫✫✫✫

49 CARS AND MOTORCYCLES

GIRATO MERCEDES 230 SE 4000

Size Length: 9.3in (235mm) Width: 3.9in (100mm)
Height: 2.8in (72mm)

Colors Original model: red, white
Replica: silver, dark blue

Price Mint boxed original, $350
New replica, about $115

Rarity Original examples quite rare ★☆☆

Schuco chose plastic for the Girato Mercedes, introduced in 1967, although while the body of the Mercedes is molded from plastic, it is actually painted, and the molding almost looks like metal. The base plate, however, is made from tinplate in the usual Schuco manner, as are the diecast metal bumpers, grille and windshield surround. Power for the car remains clockwork.

The main feature of the Girato is its floor mounted H-pattern gearshift, providing four forward speeds, neutral and reverse. A hand brake is mounted on the tinplate dashboard. The Girato is steered with the steering wheel, and there is no provision for remote steering. Both front doors open, and the front seats recline.

Production of the original Girato came to an end in the early 1970s, but Schuco has been producing a very fine replica since 1995, using the original tooling. Of all the current Schuco replicas, this is one of the truest. The tinplate dashboard is actually folded from original 1960s printed tin sheets. Today, original examples of the Girato are quite scarce and are sought after by collectors.

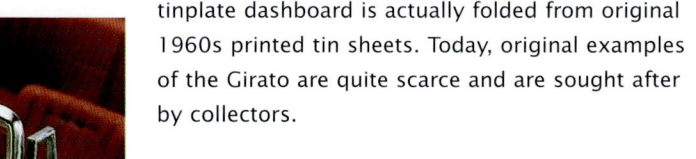

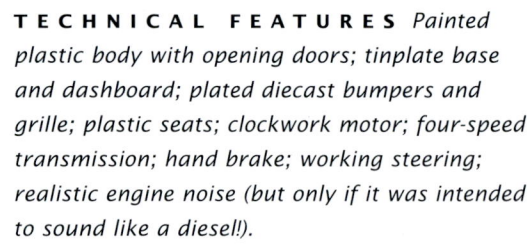

TECHNICAL FEATURES *Painted plastic body with opening doors; tinplate base and dashboard; plated diecast bumpers and grille; plastic seats; clockwork motor; four-speed transmission; hand brake; working steering; realistic engine noise (but only if it was intended to sound like a diesel!).*

CARS AND MOTORCYCLES   50

CARS AND MOTORCYCLES

BMW 327 CABRIO AND MERCEDES 170V LIMOUSINE

BMW 327

Size Length: 9.8in (250mm)
Width: 3.5in (90mm) Height: 3.1in (80mm)

Colors Cream and black, gray and dark blue, dark green and black, mid-blue and black, light green and dark green, white

Price New, approximately $100

Rarity Not rare ☆

Both the BMW 327 and Mercedes 170V are completely new additions to the Schuco range, and in no way are based on previous issues. Introduced in the late 1990s, these large 1:18-scale tinplate cars come in many different versions. The BMW is available as a coupe or cabriolet in a wide range of period two-tone color schemes. The Mercedes can be bought as a standard sedan, sedan with woodgas generator, cabriolet, police car, panel van, pickup, and tanker truck. The van and pickup versions are regularly given new liveries as limited editions. Following the Schuco tradition, both vehicles are clockwork powered and have adjustable steering.

It remains to be seen whether or not these models become collectable and perhaps increase in value. As with all new Schuco items, prices do seem to vary enormously from supplier to supplier; it is always worth shopping around and maybe doing a bit of searching on the Internet for the best price.

TECHNICAL FEATURES *Pressed and painted tinplate construction; finely printed base plate showing engine and chassis detail; diecast grille and chrome plated tin trim; strong clockwork motor; working steering, adjustable at the front wheels; removable wheels and tires.*

CARS AND MOTORCYCLES 52

MERCEDES 170V

Size Length: 9.6in (245mm)
Width: 3.7in (95mm) Height: 3.4in (88mm)

Colors Sedan: black, gray (woodgas),
dark red and black, green (police), khaki (Desert Fox)

Price New, about $100

Rarity Not rare ☆

53 CARS AND MOTORCYCLES

GRAND PRIX RACER 1070/1

Size Length: 6.3in (160mm) Width: 3.7in (95mm) Height: 2.3in (58mm).

Colors Burnt orange, red, blue, silver, yellow, dark green and yellow, chrome

Price Good to mint boxed original example, $100–200 Replica, new from $40; earlier mint boxed, $100

Rarity Medium ★★☆

First produced in 1955 and based on the Formula One Ferrari of the day, this toy went on to become a real Schuco classic and probably the company's most popular product in the early 1960s. Very chunky and sturdy in construction, this delightful model is still made today, using the original 1950s tooling.

Fitted with a fast and long-running clockwork motor, the Grand Prix Racer needs a lot of floor space to make the most of its impressive performance, but in case of accidents, a rubber bumper is provided to protect the furniture. The motors seem to last forever, and the only likely problems are missing mirrors and windshields. For quick pit-stops, Schuco provides a jack, wrenches, tire lever, and hammer, and the company continues to update the model with new color schemes.

TECHNICAL FEATURES Long-running clockwork motor; working hand brake; rack-and-pinion steering; removable wheels and tires.

CHRONOLOGY

○ ○ ○

1954 Introduced, available in red, silver, blue and burnt orange with a gray base plate.

1966 Production stopped following Schuco's demise.

1988 Reintroduced by Gama.

1990s Regular introduction of limited-edition versions.

1994 Yellow Ferrari-badged example produced.

1995 Fully chromed model produced.

1997 New Grand Prix set released to commemorate the founding of Schreyer and Co. Included a one-off Racer, a set of galvanized tools, and a Swiss-made wristwatch with stopwatch and interval timing among other features. Also released, a compatible Studio 1050 with a Racing Support Team consisting of driver, timekeeper, three mechanics, and team manager.

2000 Green and yellow version produced.

2001 Special red version with black and white checkered band produced.

CARS AND MOTORCYCLES

MERCEDES STUDIO 1050

Size Length: 5.5in (140mm)
Width: 3.3in (85mm) Height: 2.4in (60mm)

Colors Silver, red, dark blue, light green, light turquoise

Price Mint boxed early example, $400

Rarity Medium ★★

Introduced as long ago as 1936, and still being made today, the Studio Mercedes was way ahead of its time as a toy, and undoubtedly it is the most well-known model that Schuco ever produced. Based on the legendary Mercedes "Silver Arrow" Grand Prix racer, the Schuco version was put together from 101 individual components and, at the height of production, the Schuco factory was assembling 8,000 cars daily. Oddly enough, original examples of the Studio are no more common than many other Schuco toys made in far fewer numbers.

Technically, there was much to keep the young owner amused. Clockwork powered, the car can be wound in two ways: conventionally, using the key, or by pushing down on the rear of the car and pulling back. This brings a rubber wheel into contact with the surface, which winds the motor as it rotates. The working differential gear on the rear axle is visible through an opening in the base plate, as is the gearing on the rack-and-pinion steering. The latter is operated by the steering wheel, which is removable. The wheels and tires can be removed using the jack, hammer, wrenches, and tire lever provided.

Studios from this period are particularly attractive, being painted in soft pastel colors with solid colored, rather than spoked, wheels. Both sets of wheels are colored differently on each side and are reversible.

Likely problems will be hard and cracked tires, and hard and perhaps distorted rubber on the motor winding wheel. Motors invariably last well. Diecast wheel hubs sometimes suffer from metal fatigue. However, it should not prove too difficult to find a good preserved example. Replicas were first produced by Gama, and the model continues to be made by Schuco. With a break between the old and new Schuco companies, the Studio Mercedes has been in production for an incredible 62 years.

TECHNICAL FEATURES *Pressed and painted tinplate body; diecast wheel hubs; removable tinplate wheel rims; removable rubber tires; very fast clockwork motor; working differential; working rack-and-pinion steering.*

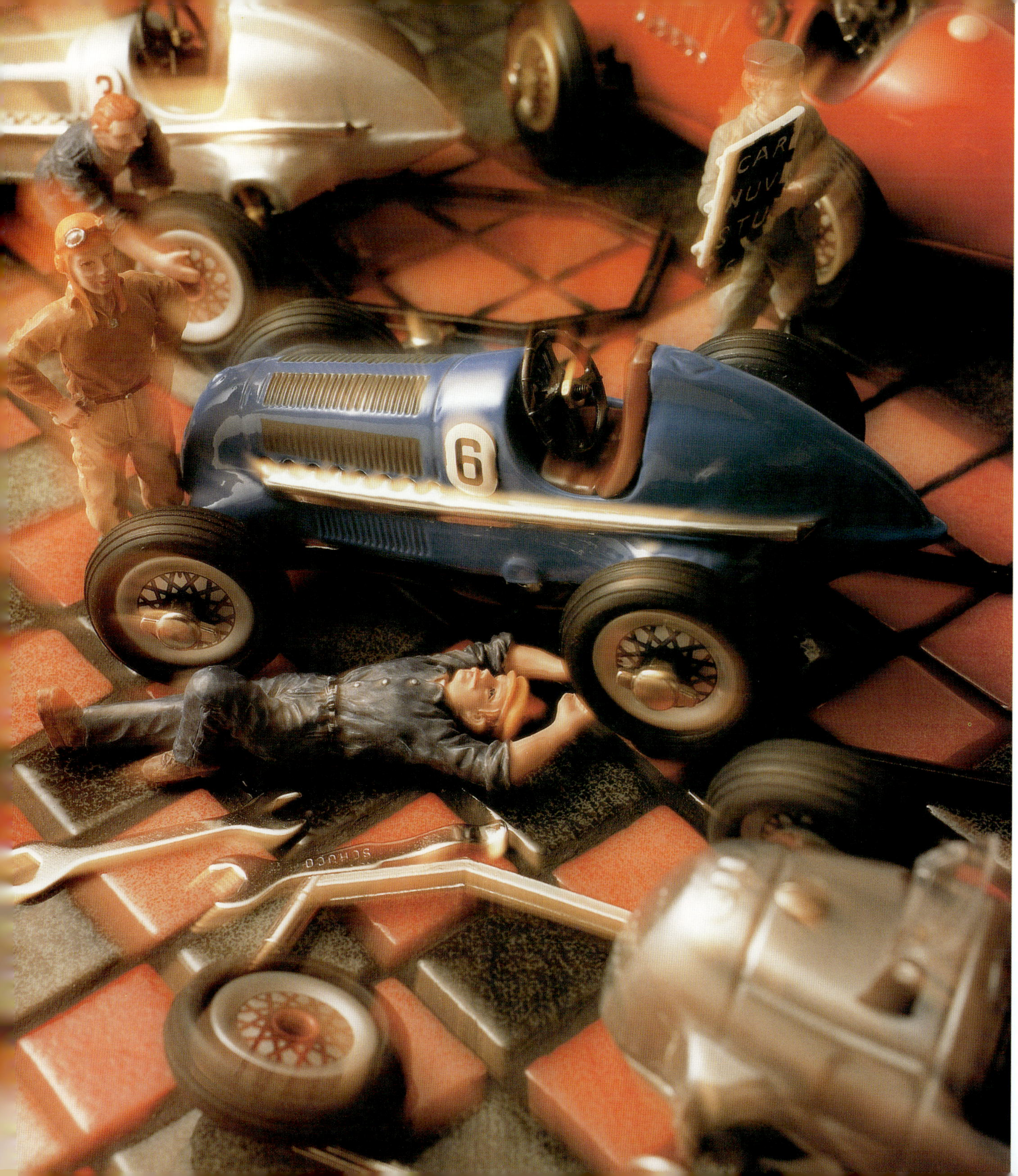

STUDIO II, III, IV, V, AND VI

Colors Auto Union Studio II: silver, red
Streamlined Mercedes Studio III: silver, dark blue
Bugatti Studio IV: red, Bugatti blue
Mercedes SSK/L Studio V: white, black
Streamlined Auto Union Studio VI: silver
From time to time, Schuco produces special chrome plated versions of individual models in the Studio range.

Schuco has continued to extend the Studio range, and currently it is on number six. Of course, these are entirely new models, although the engine, differential, and wheels are the same as in the original Mercedes Studio (page 56), hence the use of the Studio name.

Studio II is based on the famous 3 litre Auto Union Type C, as driven by the legendary Tazio Nuvolari. **Studio III** is modeled on the 1954 Mercedes W196 streamlined race car, made famous by Juan Manuel Fangio. **Studio IV** represents the beautiful blue Bugatti Type 35B. **Studio V** is based on the powerful six-cylinder, 7 litre Mercedes-Benz SSK/L of 1928, which achieved an incredible top speed of 192mph. **Studio VI** is Schuco's version of the enclosed-wheel streamlined Auto Union.

TECHNICAL FEATURES *All cars in the Studio range are identical technically to the original: clockwork motor with dual winding; visible differential; working steering. The base plates of the new models are attractively printed to represent chassis and, in some cases, engine detail.*

Right Schuco Studio 111 Mercedes W196, and **above,** with Schuco pit crew.

CARS AND MOTORCYCLES

CARS AND MOTORCYCLES

CARS AND MOTORCYCLES 60

Left Schuco Studio II 3 litre Auto Union Type C.

Above Special red edition Bugatti Type 35B, also available in Bugatti blue.

CARS AND MOTORCYCLES

THE VARIANTO SYSTEM

In 1951, Schuco introduced its new patented Varianto range, calling it "varied, interesting and simple." Varianto was a complete traffic system of vehicles (both clockwork and electric), guide wires and rods, intersections, crossings, and elevated sections. The system is similar in principle to slot cars, except that Varianto vehicles are guided by wires rather than slots. The advantage of employing flexible guide wires is that the user decides the layout. To quote the instructions, "Layouts can be built and taken apart quickly, and what is particularly fascinating is the way they can be constantly changed. Interesting layouts are possible even in restricted space; they can weave round table and chair legs, so that these are no obstacle. Varianto cars are guided by their grooved guide wheel which runs on flexible or rigid guide wires that can be arranged in any pattern, as well as on the guide rails incorporated in the speedway and elevated-speedway sections. Many Varianto enthusiasts like to build a permanent layout fixed on a board, with buildings, hills, etc. and use it like a model railway—but the real idea of Varianto is that you can constantly rearrange your units to make fresh layouts and give your imagination free play."

The range of Schuco Varianto accessories, track sections and buildings is huge. The following pages concentrate on the popular vehicles. In common with all Schuco toys, everything generally has to "do something," and the various Varianto buildings and gas stations are no exception. Take the wonderful Espresso Snack Bar 3068, which is beautifully lithographed on both the outside and the interior. Drive up to this, stop and the waitress will move to the door to take your order! There are tunnels, a customs checkpoint with automatic gate, pedestrian crossings, working traffic lights, working street lights, street maps, an automatic traffic control, and

CARS AND MOTORCYCLES   62

numerous track sections. The Gas Station 3055 actually recharges the batteries of the electric vehicles and provides them with a further 150 running hours.

Varianto production ended in the early 1960s. The Varianto range was very popular and made in large numbers, and many boxed sets have survived. Occasionally an untouched old stock store set will turn up on an Internet auction site.

Varianto vehicles are easily obtained in average, good, and mint condition. Electric vehicles are slightly rarer than clockwork versions. Unfortunately, batteries did leak in those days and they were often left in place to do their damage, quickly corroding the battery compartment, and often eating right through to the base plate.

Opposite Varianto Limos seen on track intersection.

Below Varianto Bus Limo (left) and Lasto (right).

VARIANTO LIMO 3041

Size Length: 4.3in (110mm)
Width: 1.7in (42mm) Height: 1.6in (40mm)

Colors Red, maroon, light blue, mid-blue, dark blue, mid-green, dark green, turquoise, cream, gray

Price Mint boxed, $170

Rarity Not rare ☆

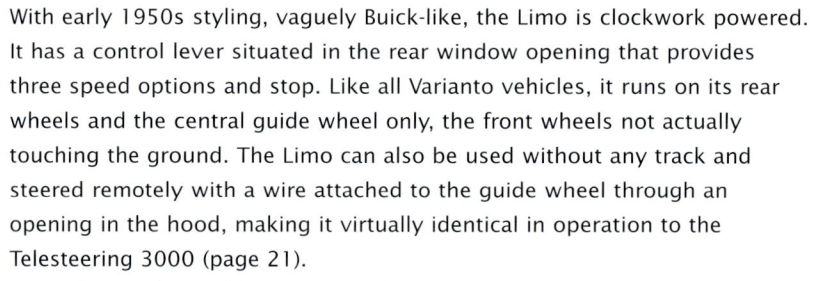

With early 1950s styling, vaguely Buick-like, the Limo is clockwork powered. It has a control lever situated in the rear window opening that provides three speed options and stop. Like all Varianto vehicles, it runs on its rear wheels and the central guide wheel only, the front wheels not actually touching the ground. The Limo can also be used without any track and steered remotely with a wire attached to the guide wheel through an opening in the hood, making it virtually identical in operation to the Telesteering 3000 (page 21).

An almost identical body is used for the rarest of all Variantos, the black police patrol car. In this case, however, the speed control lever is on the rear right fender rather than in the rear window. The police car comes from the very rare Highway Patrol set, which was inspired by the TV show of the same name. In good condition, this set can fetch around $1,000.

TECHNICAL FEATURES *Pressed and painted tinplate body with "Schuco" stamped into trunk lid; plated grille and headlights; lithographed tinplate base plate; plastic guide wheel; rubber-tired rear wheels.*

CARS AND MOTORCYCLES 64

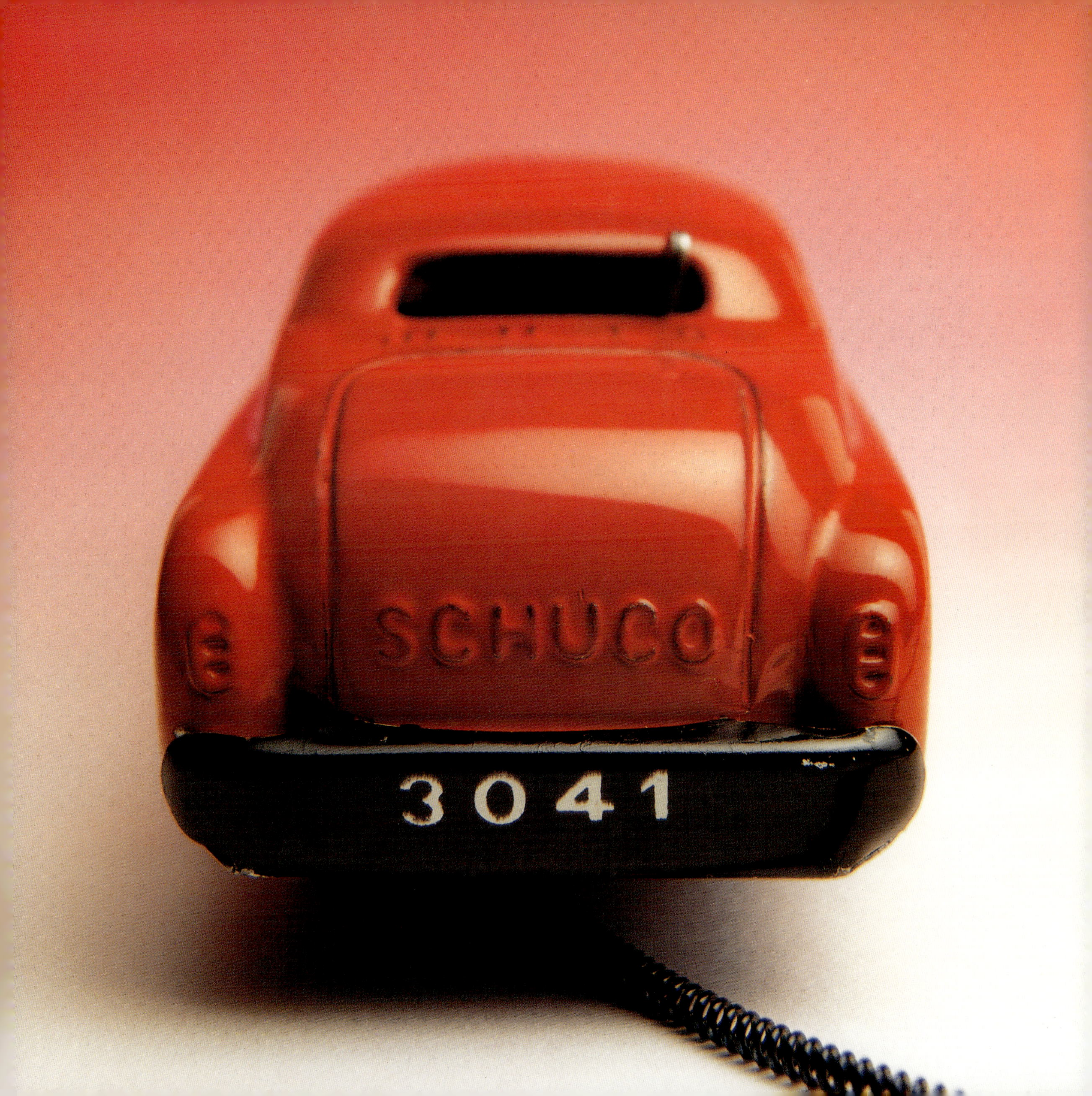
SCHÜCO
3041

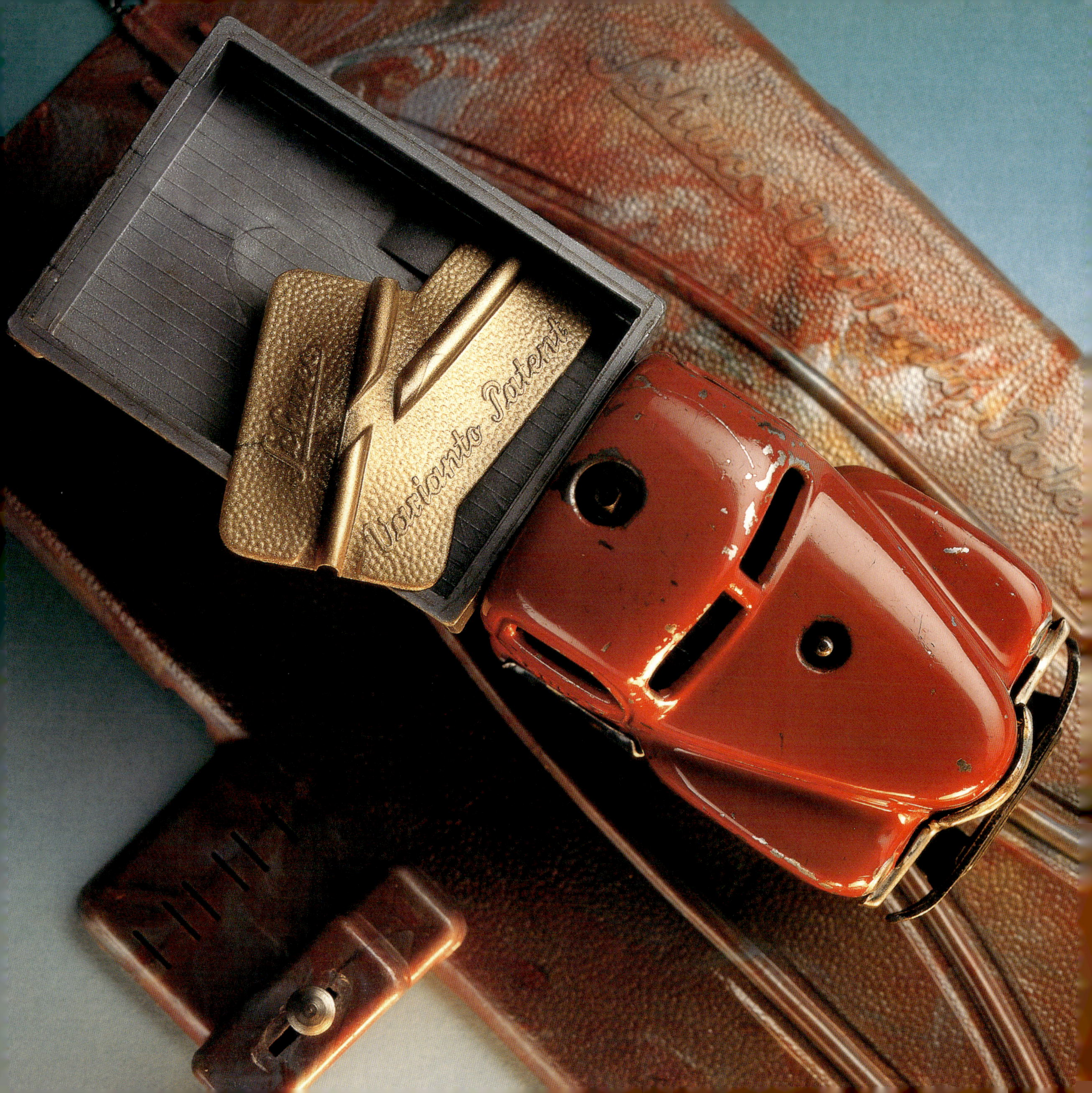
Varianto Patent

VARIANTO LASTO 3042

The Varianto Lasto pickup, like the Limo with its late 1940s/early 1950s styling, is clearly intended to look American. It was available in two versions: the clockwork Lasto 3042 and the Elektro Lastwagen 3112. The clockwork version is technically identical to the Limo, having three speeds. The battery powered model carries its batteries in the pickup bed and has only one speed option—on or off. The front bumper of the electric truck is spring loaded and pivots in the middle to act as a switch. If the truck comes into contact with an obstacle, power is shut off. Contacts on the roof allow the truck's batteries to be "gassed up" at the Varianto service station.

Lastos are not particularly rare. Not much can go wrong with the clockwork version, but the electric version tends to be temperamental, with dirty contacts and faulty motor brushes being the causes of potential problems.

TECHNICAL FEATURES *Pressed and painted tinplate cab and chassis, with "Schuco" and "3042" stamped into cab doors; plated grille and headlights; plastic pickup bed; lithographed base plate; plastic guide wheel; rubber-tired rear wheels.*

Size Length: 4.3in (110mm) Width: 1.5in (38mm) Height: 1.6in (40mm)

Colors Red, maroon, light blue, mid-blue, dark blue, turquoise, cream, mid-green

Price Lasto: mint boxed, $170
Elektro Lastwagen: mint boxed, $190

Rarity Lasto: not rare ☆
Elektro Lastwagen: medium ☆☆

CARS AND MOTORCYCLES

VARIANTO BUS

Size Length: 4.3in (110mm)
Width: 1.6in (40mm) Height: 1.8in (45mm)

Colors Red, cream, mid-blue, turquoise

Price Mint boxed, $170

Rarity Not rare ☆

This is a very simply styled bus, with no particular resemblance to an actual vehicle. However, it does have a nice smooth shape, with a split windshield and rear window, and five side windows. A plated diecast Schuco logo sits prominently on the right side of the bus. It is clockwork powered, having a speed adjustment lever at the rear of the roof, which gives a choice of three speeds. It does make quite a realistic bus noise when on the move, which may or may not have been intentional.

Although perhaps slightly less common than the Limo and Lasto (pages 64 and 67), the Bus is still relatively easy to find. Its clear plastic windows can suffer stress cracks, while the plastic headlight lenses may be cracked or missing.

TECHNICAL FEATURES
Pressed and painted tinplate bodyshell with diecast Schuco logo; plastic windows; plated grille; lithographed base plate; clockwork motor; plastic guide wheel; rubber-tired rear wheels.

CARS AND MOTORCYCLES 68

VARIANTO VAN 3116

The Varianto Van has the same basic body pressing as the Bus, minus the side and rear windows. Technically identical to the Bus, it is clockwork powered, has three speed settings and the option of being used as a "Telesteering" vehicle. It was available in either BV Aral or Shell colors.

The Van is a little scarcer than the Bus, particularly the Aral version, so expect to pay more for a good example. Boxes are rare.

TECHNICAL FEATURES *Pressed and painted tinplate bodyshell; plated grille; lithographed base plate; clockwork motor; plastic guide wheel; rubber-tired rear wheels.*

Size Length: 4.3in (110mm) Width: 1.6in (40mm) Height: 1.8in (45mm)

Colors Silver with BV Aral livery, red and yellow with Shell livery

Price Mint boxed, $190

Rarity Medium ☆☆

CARS AND MOTORCYCLES

VARIANTO SANI 3043

Size Length: 4.3in (110mm)
Width: 1.6in (40mm) Height: 1.8in (45mm)

Colors Cream with red crosses on each side and both rear doors

Price Mint boxed, $190

Rarity Medium ☆☆

The Varianto Sani ambulance has exactly the same shape and style as the Bus and Van (pages 68 and 69). Technically, it is the same too, with a clockwork motor. Like the Bus, it has a plated diecast Schuco logo on the right side. In Varianto terms, the Sani is quite rare, probably on a par with the silver Aral van.

Another van in this series, which is worth looking out for, is the fire truck, in red of course, complete with blue light at the front and a ladder attached to each side. It was available with clockwork power (No. 3047) or as a battery powered Elektro vehicle (No. 3117).

TECHNICAL FEATURES

Pressed and painted tinplate bodyshell with diecast Schuco logo; plated grille; lithographed base plate; clockwork motor; plastic guide wheel; rubber-tired rear wheels.

FLIC 4520

The Flic was not actually part of the Varianto range, but nonetheless is appropriate to include it here. It is a traffic cop figure, which can be used with any Schuco vehicle. Two versions were made, one in a very smart white uniform, and the other as a British "Bobby" in traditional blue uniform and helmet.

Flic is clockwork powered and rotates a full 360 degrees several times while raising and lowering his arm to direct the traffic. At the same time, the four "lights" in the base change from red to yellow to green. Schuco motors normally run for a long time on one winding; this one, though, is quite exceptional. The instructions claim it to be 10 minutes! The particular example shown here lasted just over five, but he could have been directing the traffic for as long as 48 years and may be a little tired, or quite possibly different motors were fitted at different times.

Flic production ran for 10 years, between 1954 and 1964. The figure may also be found as part of the very rare Play and Reality 4526 driving-school kit, which includes two non-powered Akustiko-bodied cars that can be steered by means of long rods attached to the cars' steering wheels. Boxed Flics are sought after and always attract plenty of attention in Internet auctions. Expect to pay a high price for the rare Bobby.

Size Height: 4.9in (125mm) Base diameter: 2.4in (60mm)

Colors White or blue uniform, gray base

Price White uniform: mint boxed, $350. British Bobby: mint boxed, $550

Rarity White uniform: medium ☆☆ British Bobby: very rare ☆☆☆☆☆

TECHNICAL FEATURES *Tinplate and diecast construction; very-long-running clockwork motor; tinplate base with on/off switch; base plate lithographed with name and number.*

CARS AND MOTORCYCLES

VARIANTO ELEKTRO STATION CAR 3118

Size Length: 4.7in (120mm)
Width: 1.6in (40mm) Height: 1.6in (40mm)

Colors Red, turquoise

Price Both types: mint boxed, $220

Rarity Elektro: medium ★★
Clockwork: rare ★★★

The Varianto Station Car was designed to look like a typical station wagon of the mid-1950s, although like the Limo and Lasto (pages 64 and 67) not resembling any specific car. It features lots of chrome, a wraparound windshield, and a long hood with a huge rocket-like ornament. The tailgate folds down in realistic fashion to reveal the battery compartment. The on/off switch is also on the tailgate. As with all Varianto Elektro cars, the batteries can be charged at the service station by means of electrical contacts on the car's roof, and the front bumper is designed to cut the power whenever it comes into contact with a stationary object. Varianto Elektro vehicles also have the same remote steering facility as their clockwork counterparts, allowing them to be used without the need for track.

The Elektro Station Car was introduced in 1957 and, surprisingly, a clockwork version appeared a couple of years later. Both are very popular with collectors.

TECHNICAL FEATURES

Pressed and painted tinplate bodyshell; diecast tailgate handle and hood ornament; red and amber plastic taillight lenses; orange tinted windows; lithographed base plate; plastic guide wheel; rubber-tired rear wheels.

CARS AND MOTORCYCLES 72

VARIANTO ELEKTRO EXPRESS 3114

Varianto Elektro Express, a great name that suggests something very fast and futuristic. This is the battery powered version of the Varianto Van (page 69) and is one of the most attractive vehicles in the range, usually being finished in a contrasting two-tone color scheme. The very close fitting battery cover, with good shut lines, forms part of the roof and rear of the van, and slides off from the rear for access to the battery compartment. Technically the same as any other Elektro Varianto vehicle, with the same facilities for battery charging, the Express first appeared in 1955.

TECHNICAL FEATURES *Pressed and painted two-piece tinplate bodyshell, plated front grille; plated diecast Schuco logo on each side; clear plastic windows; lithographed base plate; plastic guide wheel; rubber-tired rear driven wheels.*

Size Length: 4.5in (115mm)
Width: 1.6in (40mm) Height: 1.6in (40mm)

Colors Red, red and cream, blue and cream

Price Mint boxed, $220

Rarity Medium ☆☆

VARIANTO ELEKTRO TANKWAGEN 3116

Size Length: 4.5in (115mm) Width: 1.6in (40mm) Height: 1.6in (40mm)

Colors Red and yellow with Shell livery, silver and blue with Aral livery

Price Mint boxed, $220

Rarity Medium ✩✩

The Varianto Tankwagen, in either Shell or Aral livery, is virtually identical in every respect to the Elektro Express (page 73). The only real differences to the body are the additional tabbed-in side panels with the Aral or Shell logos.

TECHNICAL FEATURES
Pressed and painted two-part tinplate bodyshell; plated front grille; clear plastic windows; lithographed base plate; plastic guide wheel; rubber-tired rear driven wheels.

CARS AND MOTORCYCLES   74

VARIANTO SERVICE STATION 3055

Designed for use with all Varianto Elektro vehicles, when hooked up to the multipurpose Schuco 5980 Transformer, the service station will recharge each vehicle's batteries up to 300 times. "You won't believe it, yet it's absolutely true!! Varianto-Elektro Automobiles will run for more than 150 hours on just two flashlight cells!!" Schuco proclaimed. The vehicle is driven into the service station, contacts on the roof connect with overhead spring-loaded contacts in the station and charging begins. The instructions state that the batteries should only be charged for up to five minutes at any time. Probably not to be recommended with modern disposable batteries, unless you intend blowing up your service station.

   The Service Station is lithographed on both sides with gas pumps and oil cans. Vehicles can be "gassed up" on either side. Varianto buildings and accessories should not be too difficult to find, the popular items being the Service Station, Espresso Snack Bar, and the Customs checkpoint.

TECHNICAL FEATURES *Lithographed tinplate kiosk section; plastic roof and base; bulb holder in roof for illumination.*

Size Length: 6.1in (155mm)
Width: 3.6in (92mm) Height: 3.1in (80mm)

Colors Red and yellow Shell livery

Price Mint boxed, $150

Rarity Not rare ☆

CARS AND MOTORCYCLES

VARIANTO BOX 3010/30

This is a very attractive tinplate garage for Varianto vehicles, but for some strange reason, Schuco decided to call it a Box. At both ends of the garage are hinged double doors complete with little latches. The instructions suggest a "Garaging game," which basically means that with the doors open at both ends, a car can drive right through, and if they are closed at the far end, it can't!

TECHNICAL FEATURES
Lithographed tinplate body with corrugated roof and "Schuco" on each door and both sides; hinged and latched double doors at each end; tinplate base with integral guides and attachment points for spiral guide wires.

○ ○ ○

Size Length: 4.9in (125mm) Width: 3.0in (75mm) Height: 2.6in (67mm)

Colors Green with brown roof

Price Mint boxed, $85

Rarity Medium ✯✯

CARS AND MOTORCYCLES   76

VARIANTO TRAFFIC LIGHTS 3051

This 1953 set is a four-way intersection for Varianto vehicles, with a working traffic light that actually controls the vehicle movements on the intersection. On the battery compartment are two push-buttons, which when operated move little red pegs on the base to either stop or start the traffic in a certain direction. The traffic light itself rotates at the same time to show either an illuminated red or green signal. The bulb in the light is clear; it is the lenses that are colored.

The base of the intersection is made from plastic with a wonderful, very 1950s, swirling pattern of red, gray, and blue. The box cover is beautifully illustrated, showing a mother, her daughter and two sons happily playing with the set.

Size 11.0 x 11.0in (280 x 280mm)

Price Mint boxed set with two vehicles, $250

Rarity Medium ☆☆

VARIANTO TUNNEL 3010/31

Size Length: 4.4in (112mm)
Width: 2.6in (66mm) Height: 2.0in (50mm)

Price Mint boxed, $50

Rarity Medium ★★☆

This is a very simple tinplate drive-through tunnel, with the guide for the vehicles pressed into the base, while the top has a sort of dimpled, bumpy appearance. Basically green, it has a multicolored sponged paint effect, presumably intended to look like the countryside. Schuco logos and item numbers are stamped into the base. It is quite a rare little item.

CARS AND MOTORCYCLES

OLDTIMERS

The Schuco Oldtimer range consists of five different models based on cars from the early 1900s. Added to the Schuco catalog in 1962, these brightly lithographed cars are still there today. The Oldtimers are clockwork powered, and although some have their own individual features, all have one thing in common. When wound and with the control lever set to neutral, the whole body will shake like crazy as the engine rattles noisily.

As mentioned, some Oldtimers have their own quirky features. The Mercedes Simplex has a starting handle. With the car wound, the handle still has to be turned to get it going, and just like the real thing, it can take some time to fire up. The Opel Doctor car has an optional power roof, which is operated by the clockwork motor. It has a tendency to be a little temperamental. A musical Ford Model T was available as a special edition in 1965. The Renault 6 CV has an opening hood to let you see the battery operated "ignition sparks."

Schuco continued production of the Oldtimer range into the 1970s, but was forced to take some cost-cutting measures. The Mercer, for example, had its diecast wheels replaced by cheaper plastic items, and it lost its steering-column mounted windshield. The Mercedes had its starting handle

Above Oldtimer Mercedes Simplex

CARS AND MOTORCYCLES

removed and also gained plastic wheels. But in 1972, Schuco painted the Mercer in bright fluorescent lime green and the Opel Doctor car in fluorescent pink. These are pretty rare finds now, and therefore potentially very collectable for their curiosity value if nothing else.

After the demise of Schuco in 1977, the German toy company Gama—once a great rival of Schuco—obtained the Schuco logo, some original tooling and some stock, and began to remanufacture the Oldtimer series in 1980. Today, Schuco continues to produce the Oldtimer range and has recently updated it with some new and attractive color schemes.

CARS AND MOTORCYCLES

THE OLDTIMER RANGE
CONSISTS OF THE FOLLOWING:

Opel Doctor car with optional power roof. Length: 6.9in (175mm)
Ford Model T Coupe Length: 6.5in (165mm)
Mercedes Simplex Length: 7.9in (200mm)
Mercer Length: 7.5in (190mm)
Renault 6 CV Length: 7.1in (180mm)

Price Mint boxed original, $65
New, check with your Schuco dealer

Left Shaking Oldtimer Mercer.

Far left Mercer cockpit detail.

Above Oldtimer Opel Doctor car with power roof.

CARS AND MOTORCYCLES

MICRO-RACERS

Colors Color combinations are almost endless. Always particularly attractive is the two-tone Ford Custom 300.

Price Mint boxed original Schuco Micro-Racer, approximately $170

In 1954, Schuco, by then famous for its tinplate models, introduced its first diecast car, the Micro-Racer. Aptly named for its tiny proportions—the smallest is just 3.1 inches (80 millimeters) in length—the Micro-Racer is beautifully made and packed full of amazing features. At a time when rival toy companies were producing similar-sized diecast racing cars that merely sat and did nothing, Schuco fitted its model with a powerful clockwork motor, adjustable steering, a hand brake and a rubber bumper. Billed as the "fastest clockwork car in the world," the Micro-Racer could actually achieve scale speeds of around 200mph!

The word "Micro" had a double purpose too, also referring to the "Micro-setting of the steering." On the open-wheel racers, the steering can be adjusted by turning the exhaust pipe. With the motor turned off by means of the clutch/hand brake lever, the car can be used in freewheel mode, enabling test runs to be made and the steering adjusted accordingly before switching the power on. The soft white rubber bumper was provided to protect mom and dad's furniture. Small enough to keep in your pocket, Micro-Racers were a huge success for Schuco and soon became school-yard favorites around the world.

○ ○ ○

In original form, the Micro-Racer range comprised:

1037 Porsche Formel II
1040 Ferrari FI
1040/1 Ferrari Formel I
1043 Mercedes F1
1043/2 Mercedes (Silver Arrow)
1041 USA Midget Racer
1042 USA Midget Racer
1036 Ford Custom Hot Rod
1036/1 Mercer 35J
1035 Go-kart
1039 VW Beetle Police Car
1046 VW Beetle
1048 BMW 503
1044 Mercedes 190 SL
1038 Mercedes 220S
1043/1 Mercedes SSK
1045 Ford Custom 300
1047 Porsche Coupe
10 Porsche Carrera 6
1047/1 Jaguar E-Type
351132 Mercedes C111
1045 Ford Caporal F2
1048 Opel GT
1049 Ford FK 1000 Truck

CARS AND MOTORCYCLES 84

On a personal note, I was given a little orange Micro-Racer by my father, bought from the souvenir store on board the famous *SS United States*, holder of the Blue Ribbon for the fastest crossing of the Atlantic. En route from New York to Southampton in England, in the middle of winter, I can clearly remember racing it along the vast decks during the Atlantic's worst weather, with ocean spray everywhere. The world's fastest clockwork car on the world's fastest passenger ship!

Since production of the original Schuco Micro-Racer series ended with the company's bankruptcy in the mid-1970s, the history of the replica models has been a little confusing. When Schuco folded, Werner Nutz, a toolmaker with the company, obtained some of the original Micro-Racer tooling as part of his severance deal and set about manufacturing his own versions. The open-wheel racing cars he produced can easily be identified by the front bumper where, in place of the usual Schuco logo, you will find the Nutz name. On the sedans, identification is a little more difficult, the Schuco logo having been removed from the base plate, but not replaced by any other marking. At a glance, the boxes look much the same, but again minus the Schuco logo. Upon the death of Nutz in 1988, the line was continued on the

Above 1042 USA Midget Racer bought aboard the *SS United States*.

Top Original (left) and replica (right) 1035 Go-karts

Opposite top left 1043/2 Mercedes Silver Arrow

Opposite bottom left 1037 Porsche Formel II

CARS AND MOTORCYCLES

Top 1041/1 Formel I

Above 1040 Ferrari F1

Right 1036/1 Mercer 35J micro-racers

basis of a cooperation contract between Schuco and the American Lilliput Motor Company, until the end of 2000. During this period a number of Micro-Racers became available in both Shuco and Lilliput versions. Recently however, Schuco decided to cease this line, a situation that will certainly lead to an increase in the value of the existing versions.

The Micro-Racers shown on these pages are a mix of Schuco originals as well as former and recent replicas. Although some collectors are only interested in originality, all the versions are equally collectable, and all have their place in the long history of the Micro-Racer. Certainly the quality of the latest replicas is in no way inferior to the originals, although some of the Nutz products are not quite so good, particularly in the steering mechanisms.

Early original Schuco Micro-Racers generally suffer from hardened and cracked tires, causing massive understeer, but these can easily be replaced. Unlike more expensive and perhaps cosseted Schuco tinplate cars, Micro-Racers were bought to be used and very likely given a hard time. Paint would be knocked off and eventually the spring would break. Good original boxed examples, which can still be found, tend to be old store stock and hence are very collectable. A particularly rare item is the Micro-Racer Rally Set, "a complete racing game with eight 3-lane track sections (10½ Ft. total length) and 2 Micro-Racers in a colorful portable box with starting and finishing lines."

Schuco also produced a range of Micro-Jets, small diecast jet aircraft with the same Micro-Racer features. For more information on Micro-Jets, see page 118.

TECHNICAL FEATURES *High-quality diecast zinc bodyshell; sedans have either green or orange tinted windows; rubber nose cone on racers; rubber bumper inserts on sedans; very fast clockwork motor; finely adjustable steering; hand brake/clutch lever. Some of the very last Micro-Racers made by the original Schuco company had plastic bodies with opening doors.*

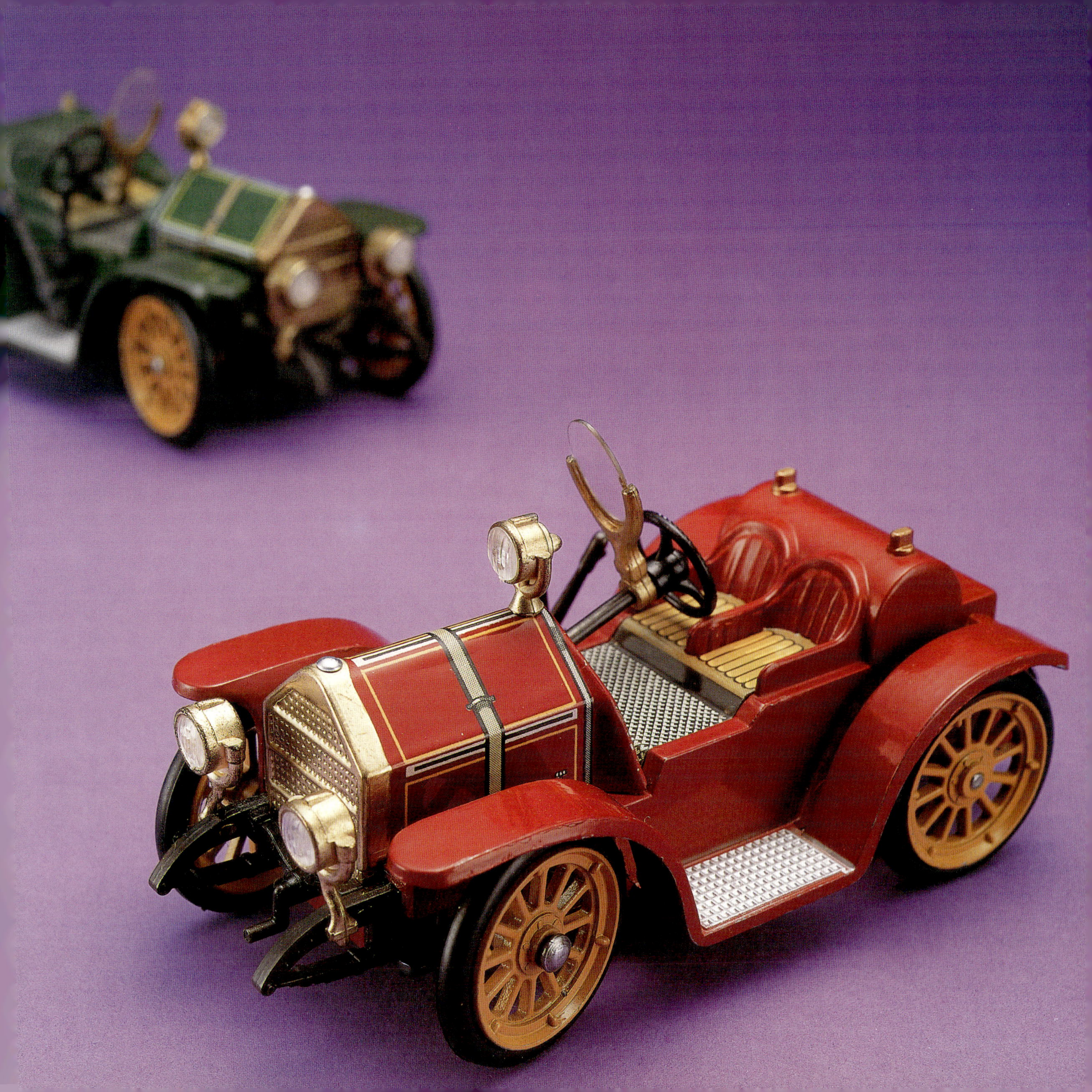

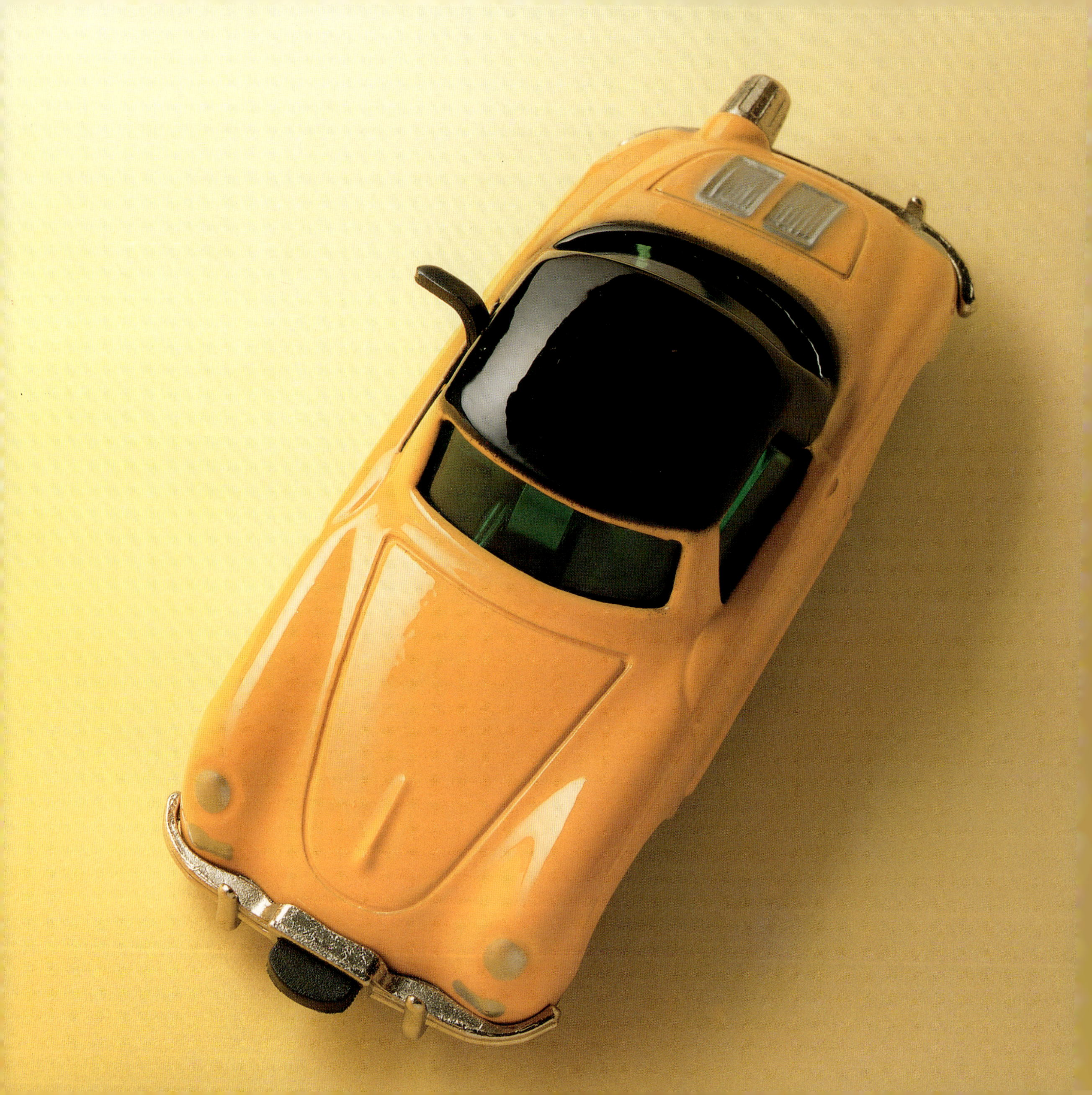

Opposite 1047 Porsche Coupe.

Below New VW Bully Box van, and 1046 VW Beetles.

Bottom 1039 VW Beetle Police car.

89 CARS AND MOTORCYCLES

Top 1048 Mercedes 190 SL

Below 1038 Mercedes 220S

Opposite Ford Custom 300

CARS AND MOTORCYCLES 90

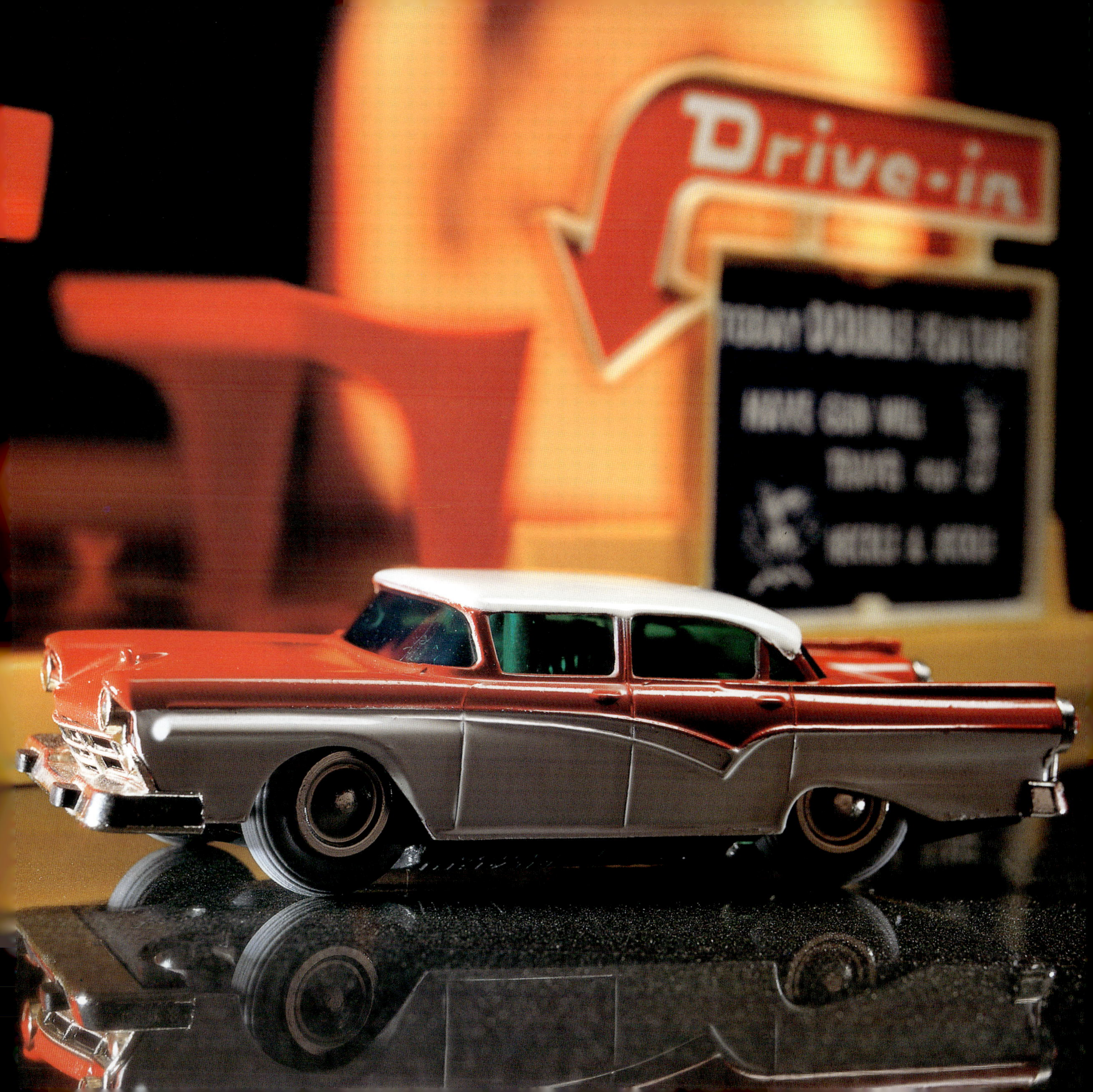
Drive-in

SCHUCO IN THE 1970S

The late 1960s and early 1970s saw Schuco turn away from tin in favor of plastic. In reality, of course, the company had no choice; plastic was the new high-tech material at the start of the 1960s, and concern was also being expressed about the safety of tin toys. In fairness, any criticism about safety could not really be directed at Schuco. The company's toys were always extremely well made, with all the potentially sharp bits neatly folded out of the way, and children would have had to have tried extremely hard to hurt themselves. It was a case of much cheaper tin toys from Japan and China

PORSCHE CARRERA RS 356 180 1973

○ ○ ○

TECHNICAL FEATURES *Plastic body (painted for a better finish); opening doors; rear spoiler; green tinted windows; clockwork motor; working steering.*

Size 1:16 scale Length: 10.3in (260mm) Width: 4.4in (110mm) Height: 3.3in (82mm)

Colors Red with white "Carrera" stripes, white with red "Carrera" stripes

Price Mint boxed, $115

Rarity Medium ☆☆

CARS AND MOTORCYCLES 92

PORSCHE 911 MONTE CARLO RALLYE CAR 356218 1972

TECHNICAL FEATURES *Plastic body; opening doors and engine/battery-compartment cover; green tinted windows; electric motor with forward and reverse; working rack-and-pinion steering operated by the steering wheel; electronic horn operated by ring on steering wheel; removable wheels; set of spiked snow tires; jack and wrench. Available assembled or as a kit.*

Size 1:16 scale Length: 10.3in (260mm) Width: 4.4in (110mm) Height: 3.3in (82mm)

Colors Yellow and red only

Price Mint boxed, $ 165

Rarity Medium ✩✩

tarring all with the same brush. Today, the well-made and perfectly safe new Schuco tin replicas have to carry a warning that they are not suitable for children under 14 years of age, which is absolutely crazy. For Schuco, the switch to plastics came too late to save the company. However, in its last days it did manage to make some quite good plastic models.

Many of the large-scale Schuco plastic cars are actually beginning to appreciate in value now, having been more or less ignored by collectors for years. Even the newest items are around 25 years old. The various Porsche 911s and 1970s Formula One cars, particularly if boxed, are worth looking out for. The BMW 3.0 CSL Coupe, with its working turn signals and windshield wiper is an excellent model and is always very popular with bidders in Internet auctions. At the end of the day, it's all down to personal choice and the decade that interests you most.

CARS AND MOTORCYCLES

SCHUCO BEACH BUGGY 355120 1975

○ ○ ○

Nutz continued production of the Beach Buggy after the decline of Schuco, using the original tooling.

TECHNICAL FEATURES

Plastic painted body; folding windshield; removable roll bar; clockwork motor; H-pattern gearshift with four forward speeds and reverse; working rack-and-pinion steering; removable extra-wide wheels; pivoted rear axle to provide a form of suspension.

Size 1:16 scale Length: 9.1in (232mm) Width: 5.1in (130mm) Height: 3.8in (98mm)

Colors Schuco: metallic blue, red Nutz: orange, lime green

Price Mint boxed, $50

Rarity Not rare ☆

CARS AND MOTORCYCLES

MATRA-FORD FORMULA ONE

○ ○ ○

One of a whole range of Formula One and Formula Two race cars, which comprised: Lotus-Climax 33, BMW Formula 2, Ferrari Formula 2, Brabham-Ford BT 33 Formula 1, Tyrrell-Ford Formula 1, Lotus John Player Special Formula 1, and McLaren-Ford Formula 1.

TECHNICAL FEATURES

Plastic painted body; steel base plate; chrome plated plastic engine detailing, mirrors and exhaust pipes; clockwork motor, which can be wound by pressing down and pulling back; working front suspension; independent rear coil-spring suspension; working rack-and-pinion steering; removable wheels. Available assembled or as kits.

Size Length: 9.5in (240mm) Width: 7.5in (190mm) Height: 4.7in (120mm)

Colors Metallic blue

Price $100

Rarity Not rare ☆

CARS AND MOTORCYCLES 96

THE PICCOLO RANGE

Introduced in 1957, Piccolos were a new range of diecast miniature vehicles, the average car measuring just 2.0 inches (50 millimeters) long. These freewheeling solid models are incredibly heavy for their size, their weight helping to propel them on their diecast plated wheel hubs and tiny rubber tires. Clearly, they were intended to be affordable from a child's allowance, much in the same vein as the British Matchbox toys. Not so now though; at the time of writing, an original Piccolo Hot Rod has just commanded well over $200 on www.eBay. com, the Internet auction site.

Schuco has been remanufacturing the ever-expanding Piccolo range for some years now. Where possible, any original tooling that still exists is used. The quality is excellent, and the paint finish is certainly better than the originals. Schuco is well known, more so in Germany than elsewhere, for producing one-off, specially liveried Piccolos as promotional models for events, as company gifts, and for product launches. In the current range—which includes sedans, race cars, delivery vans, fire trucks, regular trucks, and buses—there are well over 150 models. The Piccolos shown are all recent or new items.

Price Original mint rare model, about $200
New model, car for example, about $12

CARS AND MOTORBIKES

MOTORCYCLES

Average size Motodrill for example Length: 5.1in (130mm) Width: 1.8in (45mm) Height: 3.1in (78mm)

Price Sport: mint boxed, red, $560; green, $840
Mirakomot: mint boxed, $420
Curvo: mint boxed, red, $630, green, $700, blue, $845
Carl/Charly: mint boxed, $845
Motodrill 1006: mint boxed, $420
Motodrill Clown: mint boxed, $1,250
Mirako Peter 1013: mint boxed, $840

Rarity Mirakomot 1012, Curvo, Motodrill 1006: medium ☆☆
Charly, Carl, Motodrill Clown, Mirakomot 1013: rare ☆☆☆☆

Below Original Schuco Motodrill (left) and replica (right)

As far back as 1937, Schuco introduced the first of many tinplate clockwork motorcycles, the Sport 1012; the Mirakomot, basically the same as the Sport, followed in 1945. The latter performs the time-honored favorite Schuco trick of not falling off the table, using exactly the same system as the "turn back" cars. Production of the Mirakomot continued right up to 1964. Next along, in 1950, was the Curvo 1000, technically the most intricate of all the bikes. The Curvo can be set to follow any one of seven different patterns, ranging from a simple triangle to a complicated seven-sided figure, by turning the knurled knob on the handlebars.

The Charly 1005 arrived in 1952. This is a slightly more basic version of the Curvo, which can travel in either a circle or an oval, being controlled by a lever close to the left-hand tail pipe, with the choice of pattern printed on the rear fender. Charly also has a twin called Carl 1005, which is identical in every respect apart from minor color changes to the clothing. In the same year, Schuco presented the popular Motodrill 1006. The Motodrill, very similar in appearance to the Mirakomot, will follow a circle before suddenly spinning on its axis and then continuing in a circle again. This trick can be repeated until the motor winds down.

Schuco produced a typically whacky version of the Mirakomot and the Motodrill. The Mirako Peter 1013, introduced in 1956, has the same huge head and wild hair as the Sonny Peter car (page 26). The Motodrill Clown 1007, also from 1956, has a similar head to Schuco's wind-up figures, such as the juggling clown. The Motodrill Clown also wears a long red felt coat.

All of the Schuco motorcycles are very collectable, particularly the Curvo and the more unusual versions of the Mirakomot and Motodrill. The lithography is exceptionally fine, and the only parts to suffer the ravages of time are those that are plated, such as the fuel tank, headlight rims, and fender tops, which are often corroded. Boxes and original instruction sheets always add value, again particularly in the

CARS AND MOTORCYCLES

case of the Curvo. The Curvo was made in red, green, and blue, which is considered to be the rarest color.

Schuco has been reproducing the Motodrill for a few years now in a variety of liveries. It is relatively easy to identify a replica—the lithography will not have acquired the kind of aged mellow look that only comes with time. Although some Schuco enthusiasts may not be keen on replicas, they do provide the collector with a choice—a good replica at about $30, or an original at about $300.

CARS AND MOTORCYCLES

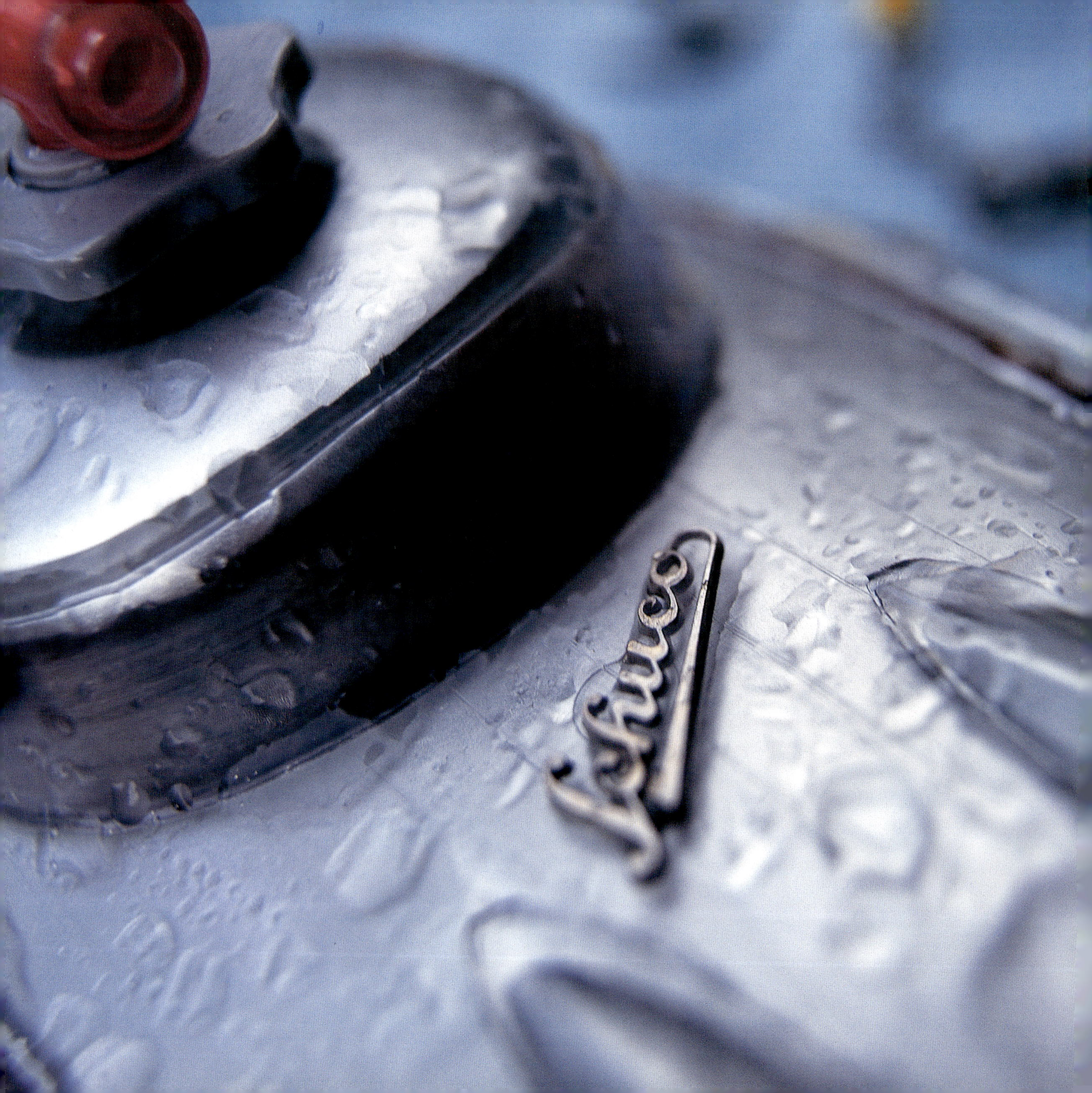

Schuco

BOATS

○ ○ ○

Schuco applied many of same features found on its toy cars to its range of boats. For example, the Teleco is basically a water version of the Telesteering 3000 car of the 1930s, with remote steering by means of a wheel and wire. The little wooden posts are replaced by floating buoys, allowing steering exercises in the bath. The Delfino is very similar to the Ingenico with its separate battery pack and remote steering.

Always beautifully shaped and well made, the only problem with Schuco boats is that many of the clear plastic parts will eventually suffer from age stressing, resulting in a cracked appearance. There really is nothing that can be done to prevent this. Clear plastic motor casings are particularly prone to this.

Shown on the following pages are the popular models that are likely to be found fairly easily at large toy sales or regularly in Internet auctions. Other Schuco boats that are well worth looking for and make sound investments in terms of collecting, are the Elektro Record 5555, an attractive speedboat with tinplate "wooden" decking and detachable outboard motor, and the Amphibio 5560, a large plastic amphibious car. An unusual item from the 1970s is an inflatable dinghy powered by an outboard motor, the Schlauchboot 7633609, which does actually have to be inflated. A very large, plastic, battery powered, remote controlled car ferry, known as the Bodensee-Fährschiff Fontainebleau, is an interesting item that won't cost too much, probably because it takes up so much room.

Schuco also produced a series of self-build boat kits, some of which were radio controlled, under the brand names of Metz and Hegi. One such very unusual item is a radio controlled model of Thor Heyerdahl's famous 1947 Kon-Tiki raft.

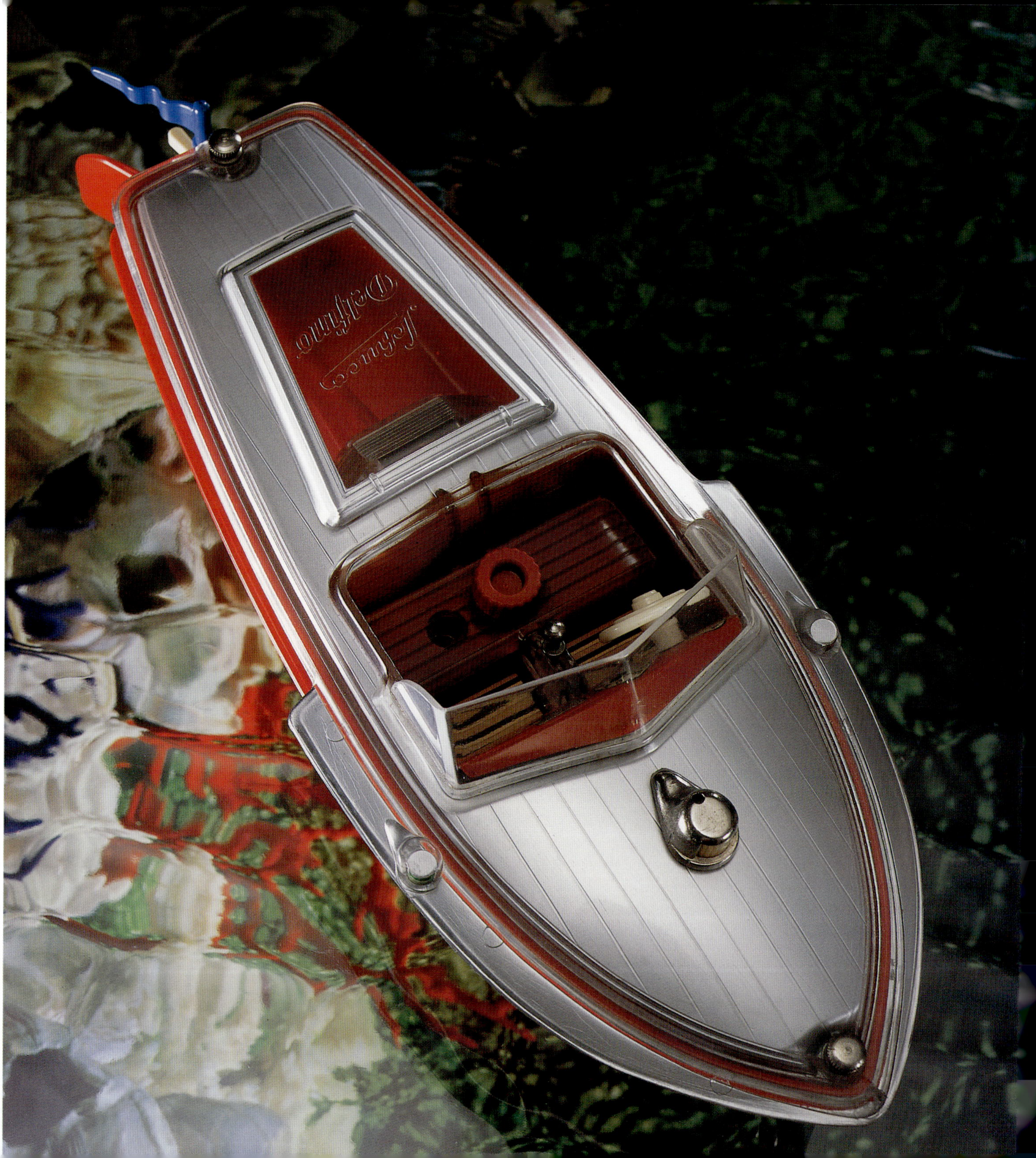
Schuco
Delfino

PATENT ELEKTRO DELFINO 5411 NAVICO

The Delfino is a beautiful and classically styled, large-scale motor launch from the 1950s. Battery powered, it can be used with either a separate remote battery pack and wire steering as the Navigation Boat, or on its own with the batteries housed in the hull as the Freely cruising Electro-Speedboat. Strangely, the boat hull has room for two 1.5 volt batteries, while the remote battery pack takes three, so the Navigation Boat will be a whole lot quicker.

The instructions include some wonderful and imaginative, if slightly far fetched, ideas on using your Delfino: "Skill Toy. Permits many fascinating water games, swimming contests, and gymkhana games with buoys."; "Pacemaker Boat. Its outstanding performance renders it an ideal boat for training swimmers."; "Ingenico Take-Apart Boat. Can be disassembled into its individual parts: any part can be replaced."

The Delfino is an all-plastic construction with the exception of the lithographed tinplate dashboard. The hull is exceptionally glossy with very fine "Schuco-Delfino" script picked out in white on each side of the bow. A throttle lever sits between the front seats to turn the motor on and off. The deck is made from clear plastic, painted silver on the inside, although a section is left clear to show the motor. This clear plastic does tend to suffer from stress with age, and it is a good idea not to overtighten the thumb screws that connect the two halves of the boat. Two floating buoys with flags and diecast metal anchors were included originally with the boat.

TECHNICAL FEATURES *Plastic two-piece hull; detachable electric motor; clear plastic windshield; steering controlled by adjustable flag plus remote steering facility; locking propeller; nickel plated steering wheel; plastic battery housing with forward and reverse switch; red and green positioning lights.*

Size Length: 10.5in (267mm)
Width: 4.3in (110mm) Height: 80mm)

Colors Red hull/Silver deck

Price Mint boxed, $250

Rarity Medium ✰✰

BOATS

TELECO 3003/4

Introduced in 1954, the Teleco is a delightful clockwork cabin cruiser. It is beautifully shaped and is very 1950s in style, with a box that is as beautiful as the boat. The Teleco employs the well-known Schuco remote wire steering system and was supplied originally with two floating buoys, one attached to the key to stop it from disappearing with the bathwater—a typically thoughtful touch from Schuco. The Teleco can be used to tow the Flotano water-skier; a blue police version was also available.

TECHNICAL FEATURES *Simple two-piece plastic construction, the top made from clear plastic painted silver on the inside; long-running clockwork motor with movable rudder that also acts as a stop/start switch; remote wire steering mechanism that attaches to the spotlight.*

Size Length: 7.1in (180mm)
Width: 3.1in (80mm) Height: 3.3in (85mm)

Colors red and silver, red and clear, blue and clear

Price Good to mint boxed, $70–200

Rarity Rare ★☆☆☆

BOATS 104

BOATS

SUBMARINO 5552

Size Length: 13.2in (335mm) Width: 2.8in (70mm) including hydroplanes Height: 3.0in (75mm)

Colors Clockwork: red and gray
Elektro: yellow

Price Both types: mint boxed, $185

Rarity Medium ★★

Schuco introduced the Submarino to their catalog in 1963. Two versions were available, one clockwork and the other battery powered. The sub is made from tinplate and plastic, the motor unit being housed in a removable pod slotted into the base of the hull. They are easily identifiable: the clockwork version is fred and gray, while the Elektro is yellow. Perhaps the color was influenced by a well-known song?

Submarinos often appear in Internet auctions, and many that are described as mint boxed are clearly old store stock and have not been anywhere near a pool—tinplate and water are not the ideal mix. However, this is a working model that "really dives and resurfaces." The instructions recommend that the Submarino is used in paddling or swimming pools, and that "if operating in open deep water (on a mission?) it is advisable to keep the traveling distance limited by attaching a nylon line to the rudder yoke at the stern. After one or two trials the submarine will carry out the diving operations perfectly. We wish you lots of fun."

In either form, the Submarino is not particularly rare, and the Internet is the best place to look. If anything, the clockwork version tends to be slightly more sought after.

TECHNICAL FEATURES Brightly lithographed tinplate hull; plastic battery/motor compartment; adjustable plastic rudder and hydroplanes, allowing surface travel and diving and resurfacing operations; plastic conning tower; brass propeller shaft housing; diecast three-blade propeller; periscope acts as on/off switch.

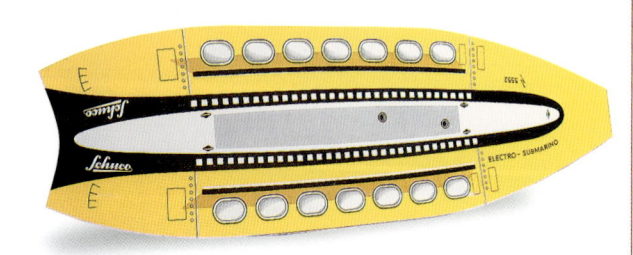

BOATS 106

BOATS

MIRAKOBO 1015

Size Length: 4.9in (125mm) Width: 1.8in (45mm) Height: 2.2in (55mm)

Colors Dark blue, red and cream

Price Mint unboxed, $250; mint boxed, $600

Rarity Rare ★★★☆

The Mirakobo is a small, but beautiful, art-deco tinplate speedboat from 1940. Clockwork powered, it was designed like many other Schuco toys to turn back from the edge (just in case the world really did turn out to be flat). In fact, apart from its appearance, the Mirakobo is not really a boat at all, but intended for table-top use in exactly the same way as the Mirakocar (page 19). Technically, it works in the same way, with a weighted front end and a central, right-angle driven wheel that turns the boat when the front drops over an edge.

This little boat is very collectable; at the time of writing, a mint boxed Mirakobo had recently fetched over $600 on www.eBay.com, the Internet auction site. Boxes are rare, and in that particular case probably accounted for around 50 percent of the price. Less than mint examples are often missing the delicate diecast steering wheel and sometimes the driver, no doubt due to the odd occasion when they did fall off the table. In Schuco terms, the production run was relatively short, ending in 1952.

TECHNICAL FEATURES
Two-piece painted tinplate hull, the upper and lower halves being crimped together (no easy access for repairs); diecast steering wheel; tinplate and diecast driver; Schuco logo spray painted on the bow.

BOATS 108

FLOTANO 3009

The Flotano is a very simple plastic water-skier, designed to be pulled along by any of the Teleco boats or the Delfino. The plastic figure, available in male and female form, stands on a single gold ski. The ski is bonded to a clear plastic float to which the tow ropes are attached.

Since there are no moving parts, there is not much that can go wrong with the Flotano, apart from the usual age stressing of the clear plastic, but then it must be remembered that most will be almost 50 years old now.

It is certainly an unusual item and not that common at toy sales or in Internet auctions. Therefore, boxed Flotanos do tend to sell well. The box itself has the usual attractive Schuco graphics and shows the skier being pulled at great speed by the Teleco and Delfino.

Size Length: 5.1in (130mm)
Width: 2.3in (60mm) Height: 4.3in (110mm)

Colors Different combinations of hair and swimsuit color; swimsuits: red, green, blue

Price Both: mint boxed, $85

Rarity Medium ☆☆

109 BOATS

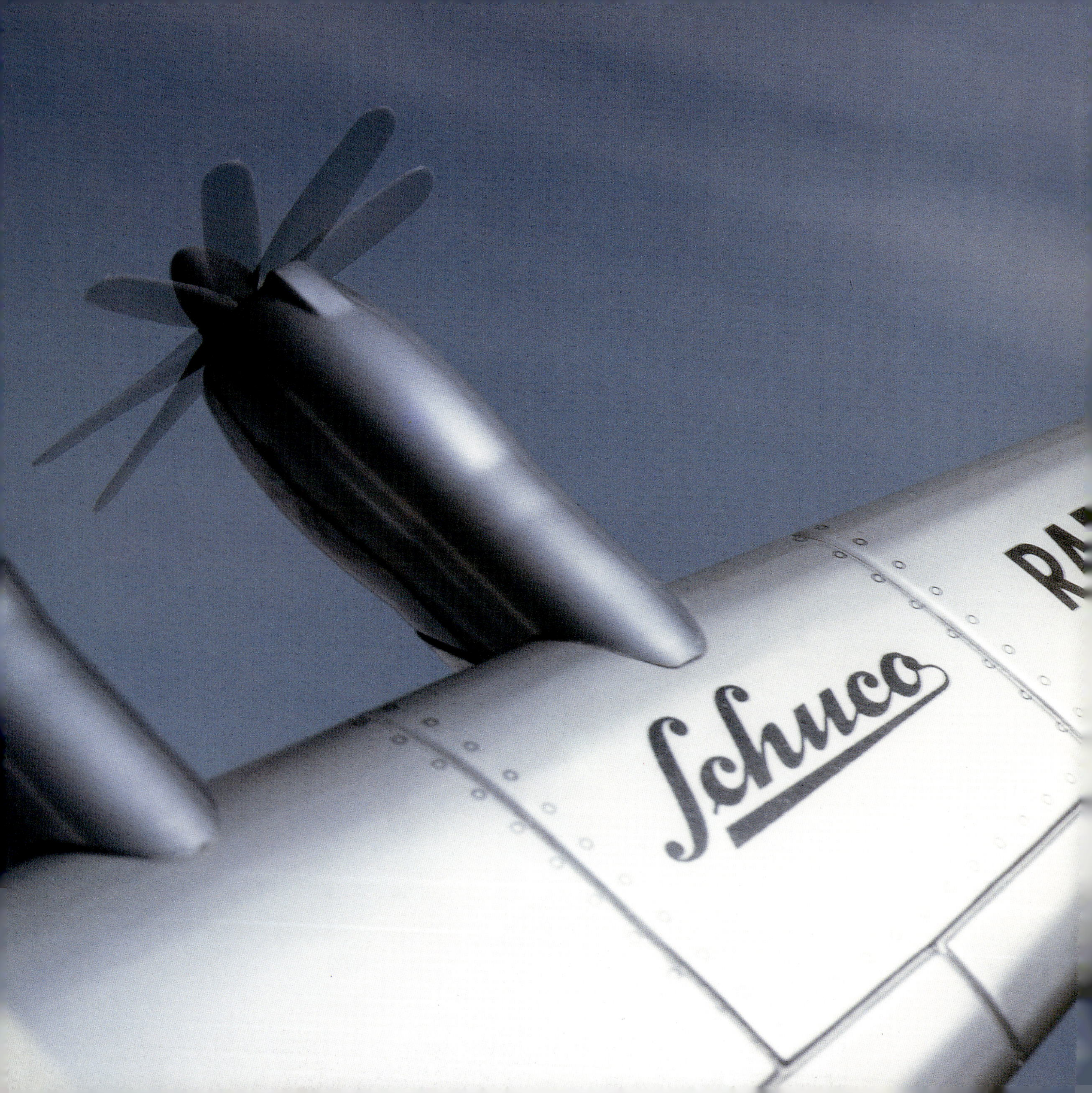
Schuco

AIRPLANES

○ ○ ○

Schuco's earliest flying machine was its 1927 Ozean Flieger, a tiny tinplate "roller" plane complete with pilot kitted out in flying jacket, helmet and goggles. Lithographed with "Spirit of St. Louis, New York–Paris [or New York–Berlin]," it is a rare and expensive find these days. It would be another 30 years before Schuco took to the skies again—but well worth the wait—with the introduction of the stunning Radiant Viscount aircraft in 1957. If there is one Schuco toy worth collecting in pure investment terms, then it has to be one of the seven different Radiants.

Around the same time, Schuco expanded its Micro-Racer range with the introduction of Micro-Jets, a range of four small diecast clockwork jet fighters. Passenger Micro-Jets soon followed, being sold mainly at international airports and aboard aircraft as tax-free items, the models being in the airline's livery.

Equally popular at airport shops in the 1970s was Schuco's range of 1:500-scale diecast model airplanes in virtually any livery. Schuco has recently introduced two very similar series known as Star Jets (1:500 and 1:200 scale) and Gemini Jets (1:400 scale). Modern printing techniques allow extremely accurate renditions of airline liveries and aircraft detail.

Schuco also tried its hand at radio-controlled aircraft, rubber-powered models and glider kits. These were marketed under the brand names of Metz and Hegi, and as such are not generally thought of as mainstream Schuco. Very occasionally unmade kits will crop up on the Internet.

ELEKTRO-RADIANT 5600

Size Length: 16.5in (420mm) Wingspan: 18.9in (480mm) Height: 6.0in (152mm)

Price Good boxed Lufthansa, $650
Mint boxed Swiss Air, $1,500
Mint boxed Hongkong Air, $2,000

Rarity Medium ✩✩
Rarest are Sabena and Hongkong Air versions; Lufthansa is the most common.

Opposite BOAC Radiant

In 1957, Schuco introduced the truly beautiful Radiant 5600, believed by many to be the ultimate Schuco toy. The Radiant is a huge model—with a wingspan of almost 19.7 inches (500 millimeters)—of the successful British Vickers Viscount 800. It is of all-tinplate construction, with the exception of the upper engine cowlings and propellers, wheels, and cockpit cover.

It is the action that is so ingenious and fascinating to watch, particularly if you don't know what is about to happen. Battery powered, the aircraft has two modes: continuous and automatic. With the pilot and co-pilot at the controls and the aircraft set to automatic, the motor will run for a few seconds before engine number one, on the left wing, starts to turn; after 20–30 seconds or so, engine number two starts up, followed by number three, and finally number four. After another 30 seconds or so, all four engines suddenly rev up furiously. A short while later, the aircraft will begin to taxi in whatever direction the front wheel has been set. The steering of the aircraft may also be controlled remotely with the standard Schuco wire and steering wheel. What makes the whole procedure even more realistic is the way that the propellers jerk a few times before they get going, almost as if the engines are proving difficult to start. Once taxiing has finished, the engines will shut down in reverse order.

The Radiant is powered by two 3D2 batteries housed in the lower fuselage, to the rear of the nose wheel. Beyond the electric motor, everything is controlled mechanically, this toy having been built long before the days of microchips. The action operates by means of a series of camshafts, rods and coiled wire. Up to the point where all four engines are running at their normal speed, power is

AIRPLANES 112

113　AIRPLANES

Above BOAC Radiant undergoing refuelling from the Shell Radiant Service vehicle.

only taken from one battery. When the cam wheel reaches a certain point, it triggers a switch to bring in the second battery, hence doubling the power to the motor and causing the engines to rev harder.

The lithography on the Radiant is exceptional, and seven different airline liveries were available—Lufthansa, Pan American, KLM, BOAC, Swiss Air, Sabena, and Hongkong Air. Sadly some of these famous names no longer exist, or certainly not in their original form.

Schuco Radiants are quite scarce, good examples in rare liveries fetching huge sums of money. Poor models tend to have common problems, such as a badly corroded battery compartment, the damage often spreading well into the fuselage; a missing cockpit cover; a main drive wheel suffering from metal fatigue and missing teeth; and faded lithography.

The Radiant can be "refuelled" using the special Shell Service Truck 5601. Contacts on the rear of the truck are connected to the Schuco transformer, and the fuel hose inserted into an aperture in the aircraft's nose to recharge the batteries. This arrangement could probably be adapted to work with modern rechargeable batteries, the Service Truck being connected to a battery charger, although "refuelling" would take several hours. When the aircraft is switched on, power flows back to this "refuelling point" and, with the correct bulb inserted, it doubles as the aircraft's landing light.

Production of the Radiant ended in 1968. Rarest of all are the Sabena and Hongkong Air models, mint boxed examples sometimes fetching as much as $2,000.

TECHNICAL FEATURES *Two-piece tinplate fuselage with upper half removable for maintenance; upper halves of tinplate wings easily removed; lithographed livery; wing and cockpit detail; clear plastic cockpit cover; diecast wheels with rubber tires.*

AIRPLANES

Above The tailfins of the slightly more common but very sought-after and attractive Swissair livery (top), the very rare and hard to find Sabena (middle), and Holland's national carrier, KLM (bottom).

AIRPLANES 116

RADIANT-5600
Schuco
START
STOP
AUTOMATIC
NONSTOP
LUFTHANSA
Schuco

MICRO-JETS

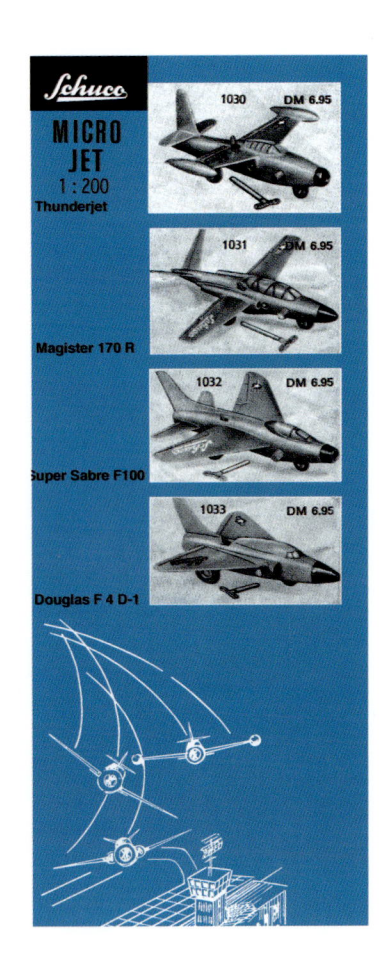

Introduced in 1957, Micro-Jets are identical in principle to Micro-Racer cars. They are equipped with exceptionally fast clockwork motors, a clutch lever for freewheeling, and finely adjustable steering.

Schuco made four different models of jet fighters in the Micro-Jet range—the Douglas F4 D-1, the Super Sabre F100, Fouga Magister 170R, and the Thunderjet. All were available in either red or silver, and each was fitted with a rubber "shock absorber" nose cone. As for the scale, one Schuco pamphlet from the 1960s claims that they are 1:100, while another states that they are 1:200.

Replicas of some models are available from both Schuco and Lilliput, cast from original tooling. The aircraft pictured here is an original Schuco Douglas F4 D-1 from the 1960s. Schuco also applied the Micro-Jets name to a range of larger passenger jet aircraft, notably the Boeing 737 and Boeing 747. These models were a combination of lithographed tinplate and plastic, the former being used for the upper half of the fuselage, while the latter was employed for the remainder. Clockwork powered, these fine models were once a common sight in airport shops around the world during the 1970s. Several different liveries were available, such as Condor, KLM, Lufthansa, Braniff, and Swissair. The Swissair 737 is particularly sought after.

TECHNICAL FEATURES *High-quality diecast zinc fuselage and wings; diecast plated wheels with rubber tires; plated steering adjustment wheel; black rubber nose cone.*

Size Length: 5.5in (140mm)
Wingspan: 4.3in (110mm)
Height: 2.1in (54mm)

Price Mint boxed original, $100
New replica, about $35

Rarity Rare ★☆☆☆

AIRPLANES 118

119 AIRPLANES

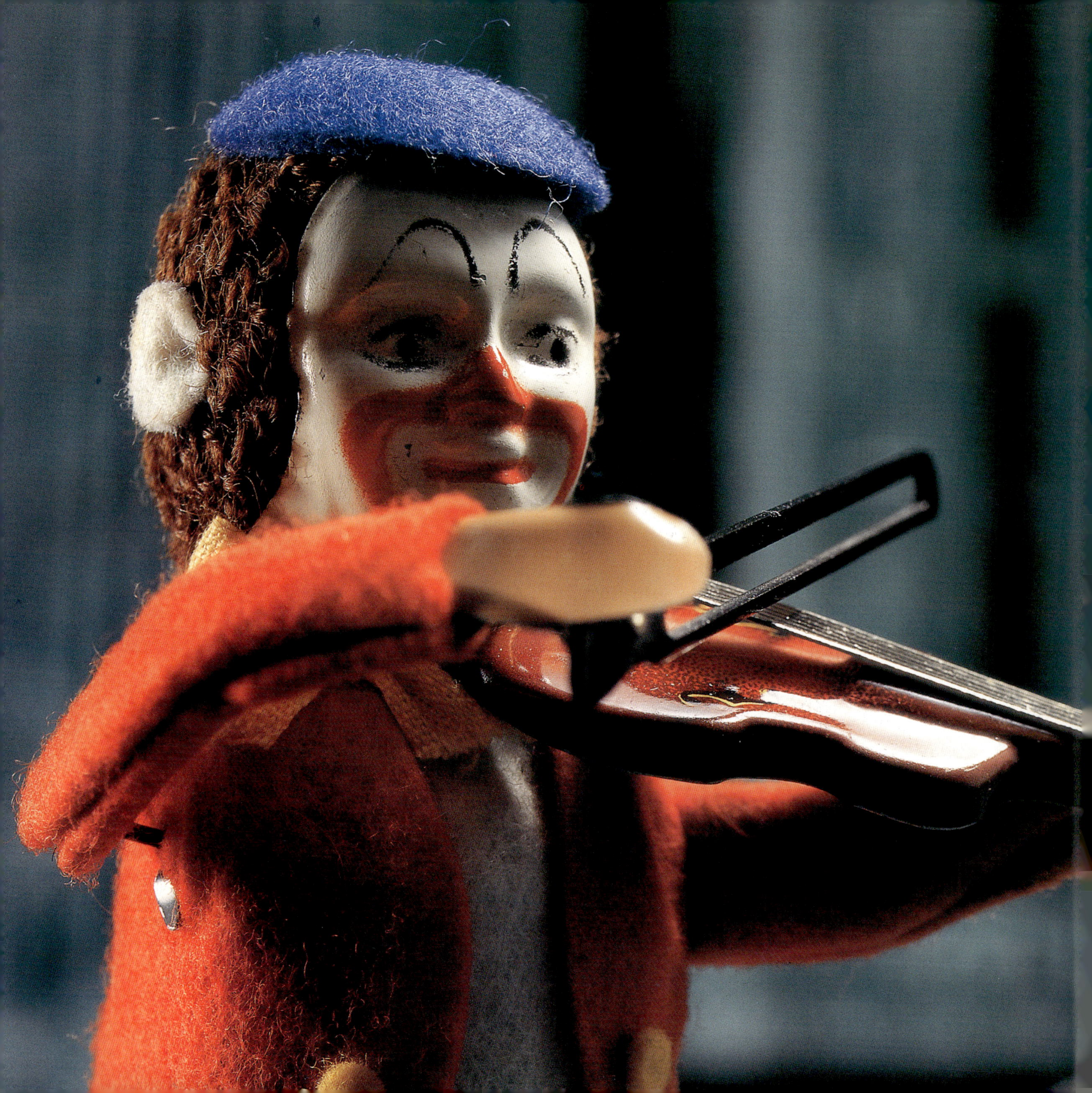

OTHER TOYS

○ ○ ○

While this book has concentrated on the popular side of collecting Schuco, namely transport toys—cars, race cars, boats and airplanes—it should be remembered that the company was originally known for its toy figures and animals, particularly prior to World War II.

Schuco made literally hundreds of plush covered tin figures and soft toys, including little monkeys containing miniature perfume bottles, "yes-no" teddy bears and monkeys, Bel Hop monkeys, animal yo-yos, acrobatic tumbling mice, a clockwork Charlie Chaplin, the famous Pick-Pick bird, a clockwork Donald Duck, a clockwork Scottie dog, very realistic clockwork mice, and a whole host of other wind-up figures.

DISNEYLAND ALWEG MONORAIL

Size Length: front/rear car, 5.9in (150mm); center car, 3.1in (80mm)
Width: 1.4in (36mm)
Height: 1.8in (45mm)

Colors Silver, red, blue—all with silver and cream side panels

Price Mint boxed set, $500–600

Rarity Medium ☆☆

Introduced by Schuco in 1961, the excellent and quite unique Disneyland Monorail is a working 1:90-scale electric model of the real Disneyland Mark 1 Monorail, which first ran in the summer of 1959 and, at the time, was considered very futuristic.

Four set sizes were listed in the Schuco catalog, all with a three-car monorail, apart from the largest, which had a four-car monorail and considerably more track. Numerous accessories, track sections, junctions, signals, and pylons could be bought to customize the layout, including special pylons that allowed the monorail to run above standard model railroad track. The monorail can also be used in conjunction with a Varianto layout, as shown in an early Schuco pamphlet, although the two scales are not an exact match.

The Schuco Monorail was offered in three different color schemes, the predominant color being silver, red, or the rarer and generally more sought after, blue. Silver was an odd choice of color, since Disneyland actually ran red, blue and yellow monorails. The main body of the monorail car is made from an opaque neutral-colored plastic, as can be seen in the unpainted window areas. Paint can be a bit of a problem on well used monorails, which can end up being very scratched; perhaps the art of getting paint to stick to plastic had not been perfected in the early 1960s. The corrugated side panels and "skirts" are one-piece lithographed tinplate items printed with the Schuco logo, the full title—"Disneyland Alweg Monorail System"— and right at the base, "Copyright—Walt Disney USA."

The monorail track has three rails, and the train can take its power from either the top and left-hand rail, or the top and right-hand rail. The choice is controlled by a switch on the train itself. Uniquely, this allows two trains to be run on the same track at the same time, using two different transformers to control them. A working headlight and a red taillight are fitted to the monorails. The rear skirts on later models were given tail fins with red plastic light lenses. It is said that this was done at the personal request of Walt Disney, to make the model look more like the real thing.

Although very well made, by all accounts the Schuco Monorail was not a huge sales success. It could be slightly temperamental, but more importantly it was very expensive. The basic set sold for a massive $39; entry to Disneyland cost a mere $1.

Prices of monorail sets do seem to fluctuate and, if anything, are not quite as high as they were a few years ago. However, these models remain very sought after and always attract a lot of interest when they appear on Internet auction sites. Even if you don't particularly want to run one, it will make a superb static display piece. The box is beautifully illustrated, as had become the norm from Schuco; it shows two monorails passing each other at greatly exaggerated height and perspective, with Disneyland's Magic Mountain in the background.

Below Later versions of the Schuco Disney Monorail can easily be identified by the addition of tailfins and dummy lights said to have been added by Schuco at the personal request of Mr Walt Disney himself.

OTHER TOYS

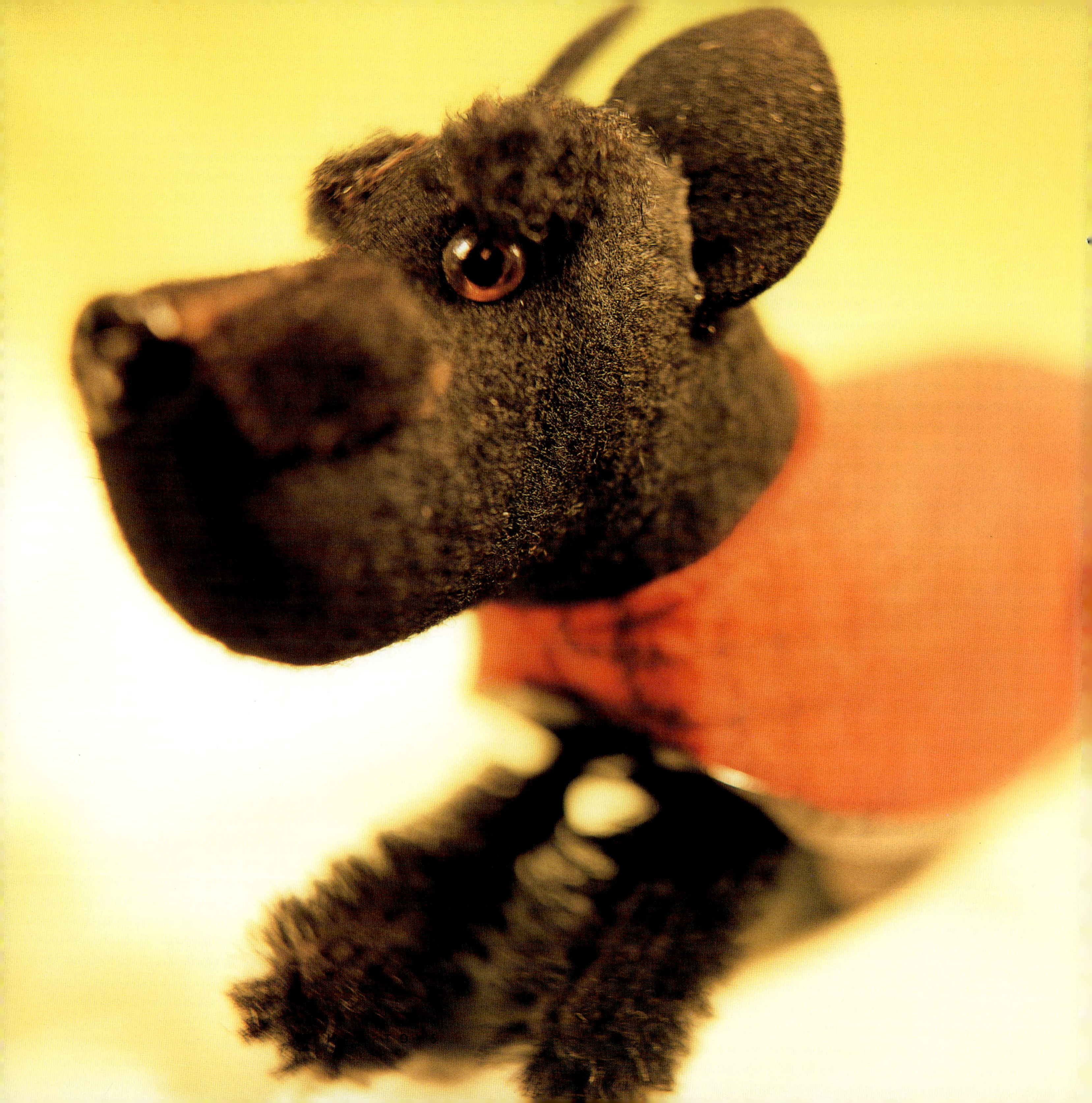

FIGURES AND ANIMALS

Schuco clockwork figures are relatively common sights at toy sales, and the variety seems endless—three little Disney pigs with flute, drum, and violin; drumming, juggling, and violin playing clowns and monkeys; dancing couples; dancing mice; father and son figures; mother and baby figures; beer drinking figures with miniature steins; sailors, soldiers, snowmen; Hitler Youth (war years only!); a fox with a stolen goose; and much more.

These little clockwork figures all measure about 4.5 inches (115 millimeters) in height, and many of them rely on the same basic function. Once wound, they will shuffle around in a circle and, depending on what they are supposed to be doing, will raise and lower either one or both arms. For example, the monkey violinist will use one arm, the beer drinker and drummer both arms. The juggling clown, cowboy, and Mr Atom—a mad figure with a globe of the world for a head, who juggles a variety of metal objects—all have their juggling balls or objects attached to thin stiff wires that sprout from a point on the chest of the figure; when wound, they spin

Below One of 20 million Schuco Pick-Pick birds sold worldwide.

Opposite The clockwork Scottie dog.

125 OTHER TOYS

Sample prices Boxed Pick-Pick bird, $140

Boxed Mikifex mouse, $70

Boxed clown/monkey violinist/drummer, $350

Boxed Mr Atom, $1,000

around. The body and legs are tinplate and covered with appropriate felt clothing; the face and ears are lithographed tin. Moths are quite partial to the felt, while if not stored in dry conditions, the bodies can corrode, leading to unpleasant brown stains on the clothing.

The drumming and violin playing monkeys and clowns are the easiest of the figures to find, and their prices are not too high. The expensive rarities are Mr Atom, the juggling cowboy, the father and son, the Disney pig with money-box drum, and the fox and goose. A good set of the three pigs is always worth investing in.

Left to right Drumming clown; Mikifex clockwork mouse; Figure with porcelain beer stein.

OTHER TOYS

FURTHER READING

Rudger Huber, **Schuco**, Battenberg-Antiquiten-Katalog, 1995.
A catalog-style book, and comprehensive; 447 pages with black and white photographs.

Gerhard G Walter, **Tin Dream Machines—German Tin Toy Cars and Motorcycles of the 1950s and 1960s**, New Cavendish Books, 1996.
Featuring tin toy cars from all the famous German toy makers—Arnold, Distler, Kellerman, Gama, Schuco, and Tipp; 191 pages in full color.

The official Schuco catalog published annually. The 2002 catalog has 87 pages.

WEB SITES

www.schuco.de
The official web site of Dickie-Schuco GmbH & Co. KG. The site shows the current range and new or forthcoming releases.

www.eBay.com
Log on to make an international search for Schuco, and an average of 22 pages of items for sale will come up. Auctions generally last from three to nine days. Some items will have a reserve, others will not. Values are given in euros and US dollars. Sellers can be emailed with questions if descriptions are not adequate. Before bidding, it is worth checking out shipping and insurance costs, and possible import taxes. As with most auctions, all the action tends to take place right at the end, often in the early hours of the morning, depending on where you live.

A general search for Schuco on the Internet will always bring up several dealer web sites, together with Schuco related photographs and general information.

ACKNOWLEDGMENTS

Thanks to Sabine Zühlke at Dickie-Schuco; Alcuin Mitchell for excellent deals and advice; Dave Deamer for help with the Radiants; Doug Burwell for helping out with the monorails; and finally to Dad for that first Micro-Racer.

INDEX

Page numbers in **bold** type refer to main entries.

Akustico 2002 **24–5**, 34, 71
Alfa Romeo 44, 46–7
ambulances 19, 70
animals 26, **124–6**

Beach Buggy 355120 **94**
BMW 22, 26, 52, 95
    327 **52**
    CSL Coupe **93**
    Micro-Racer **83**
Boeing 737 118
brakes 22, 24, 26, 27, 30, 39, 50, 82
Buick 31, 32, 64
"bump and go" 31

Carl **98**
Carreto 5330 trailer 32–3
Charly **98**
Combinato 4003 **34**
Command Car **8–9**
Command Car Garage 8, **9**
Curvo 7, **98–9**

Dalli 101 4, **44–5**, 47
diecasting 4, 82, 97, 118
Disneyland Alweg Monorail **122–3**
Douglas 118

Elektro
    Elektro-Ingenico 5311 32
    Elektro-Radiant 5600 **112–17**
    Fire Truck 3117 70
    Opel Admiral Elektro Alarm Car 5304 **48–9**
    Razzia 5509 **40**
    Varianto Elektro Express 3114 **73**
    Varianto Elektro Station Car 3118 **72**
    Varianto Elektro Tankwagen 3116 **74**
    Xpatent Elektro Delfino 5411 Navico **102–3**
Examico
    11 **35**
    4001 **22–3**, 24
    Sport **27**
    Spyder **27**
    Tacho-Examico 4002 **30**, 34

Ferrari 54–5, 95
    Micro-Racer **83**, 86
Fex 1111 **16–17**
figures 26, 44–7, 71, 109, **125–7**
fire chief's car 19, 40
fire truck 70
Flic 4520 **71**
Flotano 104, **109**
Ford 95
    Micro-Racers **82–3**, 91
    Model T **79–81**
Formula One **93**, 95
Fouga Magister 118
Gama 4

Gama-Schuco 100 **31**
garages
    Command Car Garage 8, **9**
    Varianto Box 3010/30 **76**
Gasoline Pump 5506 36, 43
gears 22, 27, 30, 34, 35, 43, 50, 56
Girato Mercedes 230 SE 4000 **50–1**
Go-Kart 83, **85**
Grand Prix Racer 1070/1 **54–5**

headlights 32–3
Helldriver **16–17**
Hitler Youth 125
Hollenraser **16–17**
horns 24, 34, 41
Hot Rod 97

Ingenico **32–3**

Jaguar Micro-Racer **83**

Lilliput Motor Company 85–6, 118
Limousine 1010 **14**
Lotus 95

Magico
    2008 **10–11**, 47
    Alfa Romeo 2010 **46–7**
Matra-Ford Formula One 95
Maybach 8, 14
Mercedes 36–41, 50–3, 56–61
    170V Limousine **52–3**
    Control Car 2095 **38–9**, 41
    Elektro Phänomenal 5503 **36–7**
    Micro-Racers **83–5**, 90
    Simplex **79–81**
    Studio 1050 7, **56–61**
Mercer
    Micro-Racer **83**, 86
    Oldtimer **79–81**
Micro-Jets 86, **118–19**
Micro-Racers 4, **82–91**
    Rally Set **86**
Mikifex **125–6**
Mirako
    Bus 1004 19
    Car 1001 **19**
    Sani 1003 19
Mirakobo 1015 **108**
Mirakomot **98**
Montage Mercedes 2097 39
Monte Carlo Rallye Car 356218 **93** spelling ???
Motodrill **98–9**
Mr Atom **125–6**
Müller, Heinrich 4
musical movements 12, 24, 28, 79

Nutz, Werner 4, 85–6

Oldtimers **79–81**
Opel
    Admiral Control Car 5309 **48–9**
    Admiral Elektro Alarm Car 5304 **48–9**
    Doctor **79–81**
    Micro-Racer **83**

Packard
    Elektro-Radio 43
    Elektro-Synchromatic 5700 7, **42–3**

Patent Auto 1001 14, **18**
Patent-Motor-Car 4
Patent Elektro Delfino 5411 Navico **102–3**
Piccolo **96–7**
Pick-Pick 4, **125–6**
plastic 4, 49, 50, 92–3, 103, 106, 122
Play and Reality 4526 71
police vehicles 40, 52, 64, 83, 87, 104
Porsche 27
    911 **93**
    Carrera RS 356 180 **92**
    Micro-Racers **83–5**, 89

Radio 5000 **12–13**, 28
Radio Auto 4012 **28–9**
random motion 12
reclining seats 50
Renault 6 CV **79–81**
reverse gear 8, 30, 34, 47, 50
Rollyvox 1080 **41**

service stations 19
    Gasoline Pump 5506 36, 43
    Varianto Service Station 3055 63, 67, **75**
Shell Service Truck 5601 **114**
Sonny Mouse 2005 26
Sonny Peter 2006 **26**, 44
SOS button 17
speedometer 30, 34
Sport **98**
Studio 1050 7, **56–61**
Submarino 5552 **106–7**
Super Sabre 118

Tacho-Examico 4002 **30**, 34
Teleko 3003/4 **104–5**
Telesteering 3000 **20–1**, 64
Texi 5735 **47**
Thunderjet 118
track 62–3, 77, 86, 122
"turn back" 4, 7, 14, 18, 19, 31, 44, 108
turn signals 33, 93

Varianto 19, **62–78**
    Box 3010/30 **76**
    Bus **68**
    Customs Checkpoint 75
    Disneyland Alweg Monorail **122–3**
    Elektro Express 3114 **73**
    Elektro Lastwagen 3112 67
    Elektro Station Car 3118 **72**
    Elektro Tankwagen 3116 **74**
    Expresso Snack Bar 3068 62, 75
    Fire Truck 3047/3117 **70**
    Highway Patrol 64
    Lasto 3042 **66–7**
    Limo 3041 63, **64–5**
    Sani 3043 **70**
    Service Station 3055 63, 67, 72, **75**
    Traffic Lights 3051 **77**
    Tunnel 3010/31 **78**
    Van 3116 **69**, 73
Vickers Viscount 112–17
voice commands 8
VW Micro-Racers **83**, 87

whistle, Schuco 8